The ONE-MINUTE HOME ORGANIZER

EMILIE BARNES

HARVEST HOUSE PUBLISHERS

EUGENE, OREGON

Cover photos © iStockphoto.com

Cover by Dugan Design Group, Bloomington, Minnesota

THE ONE-MINUTE HOME ORGANIZER
Copyright © 2007 by Emilie Barnes
Published by Harvest House Publishers
Eugene, Oregon 97402
www.harvesthousepublishers.com

Library of Congress Cataloging-in-Publication Data
  Barnes, Emilie.
  The one-minute home organizer / Emilie Barnes.
    p. cm.
  ISBN-13: 978-0-7369-2134-3
  ISBN-10: 0-7369-2134-6
  1. Storage in the home. 2. House cleaning. 3. Interior decoration. I. Title.
  TX309.B37 2007
  648'.8—dc22
                                              2007021431

CONTENTS

SHORT AND SWEET

My first series of books was the "15-Minute" series, the second was the "5-Minute" series…and now we have *The One-Minute Home Organizer*. Yes, we live at a hectic pace, one that says, "Make it short and sweet."

For the last eight years I have had the privilege to air one-minute organization hints over 220 Christian radio stations across America. These helpful hints form the basis of the book you now hold.

The book of James tells us to not only be hearers of God's Word, but also to be doers. Even though the thoughts in this book are not God-breathed, my desire is that you would put into action what you read. The reading is not what causes growth—rather, it is the action that causes change. Be a reader *and* a doer…

—Emilie

ORGANIZING

Have a time and place for everything, and do everything in its time and place, and you will not only accomplish more, but have far more leisure than those who are always hurrying, as if vainly attempting to overtake time that had been lost.

—Tryon Edwards

When we create a home full of warmth, love, and respect, it is a place where real life happens beautifully. Where people are nurtured and growth is taking place. Where you feel free to be yourself. None of this happens all at once! It's a process. As you open your heart and attitudes to God, He'll show you little ways to organize the chaos.

Everything I didn't do yesterday, added to everything I haven't done today, plus everything I won't do tomorrow—it completely exhausts me. In teaching from my own experiences, I've found that women have been encouraged and surprisingly helped. If we can incorporate simple ideas and methods, we'll have more hours for family and ourselves. Personal goals and schedules vary, but our days are numbered the same. When we analyze our use of time, especially our homemaking hours, we can determine our goals, develop our own time plan, use step savers, and try new ways.

Let's journey together to see how to put the home together in an orderly and lovely fashion. You'll discover you have more time to do the things you really want to do. Be committed. Act now and—do it!

Catch
the Vision

GET a PLAN

None of us plans to be a failure—but you've gotta have a plan if you're going to be a success. A plan helps us organize our desire to be organized, so it's a great way to start. If it takes 21 consecutive days of doing a new task before it becomes a habit—don't give up on Day 15. Are you a morning person or a night person? Schedule top-priority projects during your peak hours and routine work during your low time. The same is true for your spiritual life. If you're a morning person, then grab a cup of tea or coffee and your Bible, and before anyone is up, read His Word and spend some time in prayer. Know what your goals and purposes are. Then be ready to accomplish them!

THINK FIRST

"I've got so many things to do today, I don't know where to begin!" That's a statement we've all made at one time or another—and especially if you've never learned to set daily priorities. I have a secret tool for you to use as you set those priorities. When you're asked to do something, before you add it to your list, ask yourself two basic questions: Do I *want* to take advantage of this opportunity? And *will* I take part in this particular activity? That gives you a yes, no, and a maybe for consideration! Just remember, every request that comes your way doesn't have to be answered with a yes. It's okay to say no. Don't let others control *your* schedule. My motto is, "Say no to the good things and save your yeses for the best!"

A DAY *for* CHANGE

If you're living in a rut, maybe today's the day to make some changes! Treat each day as a treasure. Set your mind to accomplishing something new each day. A new way to conduct your meeting. A different Tuesday-night menu. Even a new hairdo! Don't be crippled by "I'm gonna," or "I wish," or "I hope." Make something happen. The woman in Proverbs 31:15 got up before dawn to prepare breakfast for her household. She planned the unfolding of the household responsibilities. In other words, she was a woman of action. What's the best use of your time and energy right now? Plan your action and get into motion!

HAVE FUN

The problem with trying to be perfect is that nothing gets done. Certainly nothing gets done that will satisfy. Here are a few tips to help you get going. Set manageable goals. Start with small ones so that you feel a sense of accomplishment, then block out time during each day to complete a task. Do it now. Remember, it's more important to just get it done than to do it perfectly later. Now gets results, and you'll feel great for accomplishing something. And don't forget to reward yourself along the way. A special dinner, lunch at your favorite tearoom, flowers for yourself. You know what does the trick! Give yourself some time off. Even perfectionists deserve a little fun!

SIMPLIFY

We all have 24 hours in a day! The trick is to use those hours effectively. Determine how much time you're going to give each activity. Matthew 6:33 says, "Seek first His kingdom and His righteousness, and all these things will be added to you." Fix this verse in your mind. Then you can very quickly decide whether an opportunity will help you seek God's kingdom and His righteousness. Major on the big things of life. Don't get bogged down by minor issues or situations. Make it a simple formula for your life!

DEFINE SUCCESS

There are two common reasons why you aren't successful! The two barriers to success are: (1) making a habit of past failures and mistakes, and (2) fearing failure. And because of these two negatives, you may never reach the potential God has for you. Do some homework today. What's your definition of success? What has caused your mistakes in the past? Write out a goal for each of the areas of your life: spiritual, professional, financial, family, home, leisure, and even health. Success isn't fame or wealth or power. It's seeking and knowing and loving and obeying—God! Look to God for the guidance you need in your life.

CLEAR *the* WAY

Life will be a lot easier if you adopt one simple rule. If you bring something in—something else has to go. How many shoes do you actually need? Or purses? Or pieces of jewelry? Take a look in your closet. If it's like mine, it could use a little pruning here and there. When you buy something new or receive something as a present—be ruthless in eliminating something else. It not only keeps your closets less cluttered, it sets a different priority for things. And more than likely there's someone you know who'd love that leather purse you rarely use anymore. When we get mired down with our stuff, life gets complicated. When we release things, we have more freedom.

MAKE IT MANAGEABLE

If this is one of those days when you'd just as soon crawl back into bed with the covers over your head, read on! All you need to do is take one step at a time. The day ahead may seem overwhelming, so break it down into doable tasks! It won't be nearly as overwhelming. And what I've found is, things get done! Not perfectly, for sure—but "done" is good enough for right now. Make your list. What needs to be accomplished today—for sure? What can wait until tomorrow? With your list in hand—do it! One step at a time. Proverbs 14:15 says, "The naive believes everything, but the sensible man considers his steps." Sounds simple enough to me.

TIDY UP

I admit it, I'm a neatnik. My husband, Bob, says I'll die with a broom in my hand. He's right. I love that sense of getting my home in order. And as much as Bob teases me, he thoroughly enjoys our comfortable and clean home. But cleanliness isn't the point. What I want to do is create a comfortable nest where people I love can work and play and relax without worrying about whether or not they'll catch a cold from an unwashed glass or be faced with a pile of undone laundry or junk sitting around. Do you want to know the perfect Father's Day gift for that husband of yours? Make him comfortable. Add those little touches that make a house feel like home. It's simple! Although I must admit—keeping it that way is the tricky part!

CLEAR *the* CLUTTER

Did you make your bed this morning? No, it's not your mother speaking! Okay, so I'm from a generation that makes the bed—*every* morning. Frankly, a made-up bed is so much more welcoming at the end of a hard day than a tangle of sheets and blankets. The message here isn't about an unmade bed; it's about clutter. A wise person once said, "Clutter wearies the spirit, and fights against serenity." And these days there's enough clutter of heart and home to last a lifetime. It's so much nicer to order your day so that you have time for the really important things God has for you to do. We all need a place where we can rest and relax and refresh ourselves—spiritually *and* physically.

MAKE ROOM

Be honest, just how many plastic bags do you have folded together in that kitchen drawer? And what about all those magazines stacked beside your bed? And who of us doesn't have a "fat wardrobe" and a "thin wardrobe"—just in case? The things we liked years ago are not what we like today. Then why hang on to them? Maybe it's time to do a little cleanup. Get some boxes and start labeling and storing away only the more important items you need to find quickly and easily. Take those clothes you haven't worn in a year to a local charity; let someone use them instead of just letting them hang in your closet. The point is—you need room to grow, to try new things. Make room for the new you.

DIVIDE *and* CONQUER

"Why do it now? There's always tomorrow." This may seem like a simple way to lead your life, but procrastination won't accomplish much. Believe me, it is the universal effectiveness killer. It takes an enormous toll. We say things like "I hope," or "I wish." How frustrating—and how negative! If that's where you find yourself, here are some simple tips to get going. First, make little tasks out of big ones. Hardly anything is really hard if you divide it into small jobs. Make a commitment to someone, and ask your friend to hold you accountable. And trust me—rewards work just fine for staying motivated. Give yourself deadlines. Resolve to make every day count. Be a woman of action. Treat each day as precious. The truth is, when it's gone, it never comes back!

EVENING'S PREPARATION

Time management isn't just keeping busy or juggling multiple tasks—it's finding God's focus for you! The first step in managing time is acknowledging that you have it! Yep—it's the same 24 hours in everyone's day. By using small bits of time faithfully, you can accomplish great things. To the Hebrews, a day began in the evening—with rest, family fellowship, and study and meditation in God's Word. Devote the evening hours to quiet rest and reflection. Prepare yourself in the evening for the coming day. Even if you only manage to do this one evening a week, it will be worth it. You'll discover rest and renewal, and you will find a new way to order your priorities. This can be one of the most fruitful ways to get organized and focused.

SHARE *the* LOAD

My friend Sheila discovered the perfect solution to her housecleaning dilemma. Drowning in a sea of dust, dirt, and clutter, she was at her wit's end. Her friend Fran was feeling Sheila's pain! So they decided to pool their talents. Now they take turns cleaning each other's homes—together. One week it's Sheila's house, the next it's Fran's. Together they get a lot accomplished. And the icing on the cake—they get to share each other's company. Sheila and Fran were nervous at first. It's scary to admit to someone else that your house isn't perfectly clean—but the results are more than worth the risk! They began to enjoy the honesty and the camaraderie of their arrangement. Consider sharing the load of cleaning and the fun of a deeper friendship.

START *with the* HEART

Being organized isn't the end! If chaos and clutter in your home and life are wearing you down—the solution isn't a whirlwind effort to "get organized." You have to begin with your heart or you'll drive you and everyone else crazy in the process. As we open our hearts to putting God first in all things, in all efforts, in all relationships, in all desires, God will show us little ways to organize the chaos. And remember, it doesn't have to happen all at once. Growing in the Spirit is a lifelong, step-by-step process. It's taken me over 30 years to develop systems that help me maintain order. And I'm still learning. One thing I can tell you—look inside first. Once your heart is in order, the rest will unfold more easily.

CULTIVATE CONTENTMENT

When you're overwhelmed, contentment isn't always easy to achieve. The apostle Paul sets us a good example when he says in Philippians 4:12, "I have learned the secret of being content in any... situation" (NIV). One way to find contentment is to have immediate goals and long-term goals. These are essential. Where am I going?

What do I need to get there? Will it save me time? Will it improve my chance to serve God and others? When you're confused, the answers to these questions help to unravel the confusion. You feel less overwhelmed. I read somewhere that "contentment is not a natural virtue"! It's something we learn to cultivate. Each time you set and reach a goal, you'll discover a sense of contentment that breeds a stronger sense of direction and joy.

LOOK NO FURTHER

I don't know how many times I have walked frantically from room to room looking for my keys! And after everyone in the house has given me yet one more place to check—and I'm ready to scream—there they are. And of course they are right where I left them the night before. Right in front of my nose, yet I didn't see them. I think we miss *seeing* a lot of things. I think we sometimes miss seeing God too. He isn't tucked away somewhere out of sight. No, He's right out in the bright light of day and in the darkness of the night. Don't give up searching. The problem is *your* seeing, not with *His* presence. God is right in front of your nose.

MAKE a WAY

What's causing all the confusion at your house? The answer is simple—life! I don't know if you've noticed it or not, but organized people generally appear calmer. There seems to be less confusion in their worlds. Less life clutter, if you will. There's nothing more disorienting than walking into a room filled with stacks of clothes, toys, and all the odds and ends that have no place in a home. Sound familiar? Life can build up around us and leave us feeling confused and unable to make a way through the "stuff." Get rid of anything you don't need or don't use. Store only what you actually need to keep—but get it out of the way. Organization can be fun. Okay, maybe not fun—but satisfying. Believe me, life can be much simpler. And you'll discover an energy for the things in life that *really* matter!

MAKE *the* MOST *of* IT

If you're a busy woman—and what woman isn't—you never have enough time to get everything done. Not with all the interruptions—all the time bandits—that rob you of much-needed minutes. The doctor's appointment that runs late. The flat tire. The missing keys. The meeting that runs late. The carpool schedule that keeps you in the car for the majority of the day. Make the best of these lost minutes. Make a call. Write a check. Memorize a verse. Jot down notes for later. Don't let resentment set in when you have to wait, wait, wait. If you want to make room in your life for peace and patience, take small steps of organization, know the value of time. Snatch, seize, and enjoy every minute of it!

BRING IT ON

I like to look on each day as a gift. No matter what pressures the day brings, it is truly a gift for you. Inconveniences? For sure. Frustrations? Yep—a lot of them. People that make you crazy? Count on it! Just consider that trials, obstacles, and decisions you encounter today are all God's means for revealing His strength. Look at each one as a teaching tool. How you respond to your various pressures will help shape you into the person God wants you to become. No one enjoys difficulties—least of all me. But I've learned to make my daily prayer, "Lord, bring it on!" If you join me in this prayer, I guarantee that you will also discover how to lean on His strength as you receive the gift of a new day.

Plan
of Action

ON TRACK

Multitasking! It's a great way to add more hours to your day. I never work without a to-do list somewhere close at hand. It helps me stay on track and makes multitasking much easier. I even prioritize the tasks on the list. And above all else, I try to avoid interruptions. In other words, stay away from the e-mails until you're ready to tackle that particular item on your list. If you have small children, your list is going to change every ten seconds—if you're lucky! Be a woman in control of your time. Redeem the time so you have energy for the important things God has for you to do. Taking your life back from the worries of an unorganized existence will give you great freedom to explore a life of much more meaning and significance.

DREAM *a* LITTLE DREAM

What's your goal for today? If you don't have a goal—it's pretty obvious that a significant "something" won't get done. You know, many times we don't achieve things we aspire to simply because we never make room for them. We don't take steps in their direction. These remain only dreams—never realities. I challenge you to make a list of five goals you want to achieve. Don't make them too difficult. Here are some suggestions to get your ideas rolling: Get the garage cleaned out in the next two months. Invite new neighbors over for dinner. Take an evening class at your local college. Create a new recipe once a month. Call a friend from long ago. See, the ideas come pouring out once you start brainstorming. These are small goals that can help you move forward. You'll start thinking of bigger goals once you let yourself dream, even just a little bit.

EXPECT LESS, DO MORE

If you're feeling guilty because everything didn't get done—let it go! If you know me at all, you know I'm all for responsibility and tenacity. But sometimes you have to acknowledge that there's always going to be something that needs doing. If you've got an impossible schedule, break up the projects into time slots. Write to-do lists, do some tasks while you're waiting in line or having the car washed. Plan menus ahead of time—cook some of the food and put it in the freezer. I have a friend who prepares her entire week's lunches on Sunday afternoon. But most of all—lower your expectations. I might be the first to suggest such a thing, but believe me…it leads to less guilt and more productivity.

MAKE ROOM

If you think you're a bad person just for saying no—you definitely have the "Disease to Please"! Stop feeling guilty every time you say no. Instead, how about practicing a few life-changing steps. Never answer under pressure. Give yourself time to think it over. Learn to say, "Let me get back to you." And whatever you do, don't fall for the oldest trick in the book—flattery! It goes like this: "There's no one who can plan an event like you!" Actually there are others. And if this isn't the right time for you, let them know. Sometimes we are so busy trying to do the work of so many people that others don't even have the chance to step into their roles to help or plan or create. Give yourself permission to decline an opportunity and make room for other ones.

TODAY MATTERS

Do you put things off for tomorrow? Guess what? It's *tomorrow!* Here are some tips that work for me. Don't ignore unpleasant tasks. Ignoring them won't make them go away. If there's something you don't feel like doing today—find a task you do feel like doing—and get it done. Give yourself a reward. Give yourself deadlines. And resolve to make every day count. Treat each day as a treasure. Be decisive. Have the courage to act. In other words—make something happen. The simple truth—every day is precious. When it's gone, it never comes back to you.

GET IT *in* ORDER

With all the priorities in life—when does the fun part begin? Here are some tips to help you set priorities that work! Fun? I'm not making *any* promises! Priority #1: Matthew 6:33 says to seek and obey God. When God is first in your life—deciding among the other stuff is much easier. Priority #2 is your family! Priority #3 is involvement in your church; however, never at the expense of God or your family. And fourth is everything else. This includes your job, your social activities, the things you volunteer to do. The whole idea is to avoid being overextended. In what ways do you feel overextended now? What steps can you take to get all of your life more in balance?

ORDERLY CONDUCT

A friend of mine has a sign that reads: "I had my house clean last week; I'm sorry you missed it!" We've all been there—for sure. First Corinthians 14:40 says, "All things must be done properly and in an orderly manner." That's quite a challenge when you're raising a family, balancing a job, and just trying to hang on! What works for me—even now—is to do a little bit every day. You'll be absolutely amazed at what happens. Start now! No matter what! Make a list of three things—okay make it one thing. Do that, and then return to your list or to the drawing board and decide what should be next. You really will be amazed at how much simpler life gets when you bring order to your days.

SORTING *and* SIMPLIFYING

Let's check out your closet! With three simple tips you'll get more organized than you have been in ages. Well, your closet will be organized at least. Get three bags and designate them for clothes that you're going to put in storage, clothes you're going to give away, or clothes you're going to throw away. Most closets are a mess because we don't want to make choices about what fills every crevice of them. Once you have made these choices, the items that remain can be organized more efficiently. Get a mug rack. They're great for jewelry, scarves, small purses. And a hanging shoe bag is perfect for more than shoes. Fill these with socks, odds and ends, nylons, and other small items that get displaced in other locations.

PLAN *a* LITTLE

I hear so many couples say, "We don't know what we're going to do next week—let alone three to five years from now!" Frankly, in order to make life simple, you have to do a little planning. Get beyond the present and think a bit into the future. Where will you be in five years? What about your children's education? Your career goals? Where will you live? There are financial goals you need to schedule now. Don't wait until the day actually comes—that's way too late. If you need some help, check in with a family financial planner. The future doesn't have to be so scary.

BE READY

Don't wait until tomorrow. Do it now! Just "fill in the blank" with all the things you shouldn't put off until tomorrow. It's so important to put those photos in an album or call that friend or have that quiet time. Even as you're planning and organizing, prepare yourself as best you can for your life, but remember it's for a purpose. Your life has purpose that even you might not fully understand. Be prepared for whatever unfolds. The biblical principle is to "be ready" for whatever the Lord brings into your life. To make the most of the time He gives you. When you live with God's purposes clearly in mind, you store up treasures in heaven, filling your life with faith, hope, and love!

BASIC TRAINING

When things are going well, it's not hard to be motivated! But when they're not—watch out! When you're frustrated or your energy is at an all-time low, go back to the basics. List all the obstacles, and then list your options for overcoming them. What do you need to do to get back on track? What have you put off that is nagging at your conscience? Just know there'll be times when you just don't stay on top of your list. That's okay. Maybe a little quiet time is what you need. Time to read a favorite Bible passage. Time to pray. Ask God to help you stay on track. And be comforted in the knowledge that God promises, "I will never desert you, nor will I ever forsake you!" (Hebrews 13:5).

BE FAITHFUL

If you're looking for the secret to success—read on! If you're like me, you want to know exactly how a project is going to turn out. And you want to know a few other things before you pour your heart into it. Will it work? Will it be a success? Stop right there! Success is really not your responsibility. You're called to do what God asks— share your faith, help those in need, live a life of integrity. Leave the outcome to Him! You may never know the results of your each and every deed, but your job and mine is to be faithful and obedient—to God's Word and His priorities. He will do the rest.

ORDER WHAT YOU HAVE

With a little order in your life, you can accomplish great things! When my stuff is a mess, so am I. Things should be where they're most convenient. Put items that are alike—together. Those things you use all the time should be in plain sight. Store stationery next to stamps, along with pens, and near your computer. Get away from stacks and piles. A simple but often overlooked trick is to label containers and boxes. It takes away the mystery of having to open everything and look inside. Give yourself a field trip to one of those stores that specializes in storage units—big and small—and either buy a few key pieces that will help you organize your most troubling home space or jot down notes of inspiration. Once you get home, you can often use crates, shelves, file cabinets, or decorated shoe boxes to generate similar results. Have fun with it.

TIME WISE

We've all got the same amount of time—it's how we use it that counts! As a woman, your biggest challenge isn't planning your *life*—it's making sure each *day* counts. My mother always said, "Good things seldom happen by accident." She was right! Whenever you catch yourself thinking, *I can do it later,* stop and make a point of doing it now. It's true that each moment of your life once gone is lost forever. Recognize this truth and how you are a steward of your precious time. Doesn't that inspire you to use your time even more wisely and purposefully? Try setting aside an hour of personal time each day. Start with 15 minutes if you have to. But do it. It'll make *all* the difference!

TAKE BACK TIME

These are the five "hall of fame" time wasters. Number 1: trying to do too much at once—learn to prioritize your tasks. Number 2: failing to plan—set those priorities! Number 3: being unable to say no. I'll wait a moment for that to sink in! When you learn to say no—and mean it!—you'll find life so much more balanced. Okay, number 4: putting things off. I say either do it right away, hire it done, or forget it. And number 5: doing everything yourself. You've got to delegate. You can't do it all. Have I shed light on one of your top time wasters? Make a change today that will serve you for many more years.

SAVING TIME MAKES TIME

Take control of your time! That may be easier said than done, but with a little effort you can turn negative time interrupters into positive time *savers*. Start now! Become a list maker. I make a list for almost everything I do. Divide big jobs into little ones. I've read that people are interrupted at least once every five minutes! Big culprits are cell phones and e-mail. It's up to you to set the limits. Determine what's important to you. We're all looking for that magic pill—the one that gives us more time. It's no wonder there's never time to pray. Or just kick back with a good book. Become a woman who takes control of her time.

IT'S a REVIVAL

Ah! Time to think—put up my feet—and read a good book! Who am I kidding? There never seems to be enough time. Or energy! The older I get, the more I value chunks of time. It gives me a chance to rethink my life. God wants us to live wisely so we can learn to balance the time we spend in quiet with the craziness that fills our days. But that means setting priorities! If you have small children—that probably seems next to impossible right now. And you're right—it's a major challenge. Think small—to begin with. Small amounts of time can be satisfying and refreshing. Use them to revive your heart and soul!

DREAM FORWARD

I like the definition of a goal being a dream with a deadline! Sometimes our goals aren't very achievable because they aren't very measurable. "I want to lose weight." "I want to learn to ski." "I want to do more Bible study." "I want to read more." These are all great desires to have. But if you don't put a deadline to them—they never happen. "I want to memorize ten verses in the Bible by December 1." Or take out a pretty piece of stationery and write a promise to yourself to accomplish one of these goals this week and throughout the entire month. Now that's a measurable goal. If you feel like you're standing still—you're not! You're actually falling *behind*. Make today the day you change that.

PRAY BEFORE YOU SAY YES

Every request that comes your way doesn't have to be answered right on the spot. By applying a few tips, you can change the way you fill your schedule. When the call or e-mail comes asking you to serve on that committee, to help out with the Christmas program, or even to have lunch, give yourself a few minutes before you answer. Pray for ten minutes. Work on a project, write some thank-you notes, make a few calls. Anything but responding yes or no before you're ready! If we are laboring in vain, without direction, or only for personal gain and not for purpose that is godly and fulfilling, our labor can lead to worry and disbelief; and even if our labor brings wealth, it will be meaningless. Make your efforts count. Every day matters because you matter to God.

GET *into* MOTION

"I work best under pressure!" If you've said that more than twice this week, then listen up! Most of us think we work better under pressure because we've rationalized our procrastination. And what's the result? Frustration. Unsolved problems. Fatigue. And often, strained relationships. Ask yourself, *What is the greatest problem facing me, and what am I going to do about it today?* The Proverbs 31 woman is a role model for us. She gets up before dawn to prepare breakfast and plan her day. We're to be women of action. Women who treat each day as being precious. Plan your action, keep it simple, and get into motion!

Making **Room for Life**

OUT *with the* OLD

Here are a few suggestions for "letting go!" I have a friend who has 40 pairs of shoes. Forty! "It's hard to throw things out," she says. A good rule of thumb is, if it hasn't been used in the past year, give it away, throw it away, or store it away. I realize there are some things that are irreplaceable. Put them in storage. The only reasons to keep things for long periods should be for memories or to pass them on to another family member. When we streamline our possessions, it often begins to carry over into our spiritual lives as well. Second Corinthians 5:17 says the old has passed away; behold new things have come!

GIVE YOURSELF *a* BREAK

With God's help you can do whatever you really want to do with your time! Setting priorities makes it happen. And making good choices! Could you watch television less? Could you get up 15 minutes earlier? We all schedule time for work, chores, errands, family, church. But that quiet time? It's up for grabs. So what happens? Nothing! Fifteen minutes here and there can make all the difference. And if you can somehow plan a catch-up day, that's even better! Create time alone to read, to write some notes, to journal. If you have small children, that kind of day may seem like an impossible dream. But take *some* time—you'll be surprised at what a difference even 15 minutes can make!

PREPARED *for* ANYTHING

Sometimes you have to be practical—have a grasp of basic information about your life and your surroundings. God has promised to care for us, but that doesn't mean we shouldn't be prepared. When you're in an emergency, that's not the time to be wondering where your checking account is located. For instance, where do you turn off the gas and water? Who's the person to call in an emergency? Do you know the location of your savings and any investments? What about your will? A lot of people these days—both women and men—are learning basic repair skills. It's wise to know in advance where things are and how they work.

WASTE NOT!

With a few simple organizing hints, you can find peace in your life! Shoe boxes, cardboard boxes, hat boxes—they're perfect for storing clutter. Plastic bins, stacking trays, even laundry containers are useful. Large envelopes can serve to organize small items. List the contents on the outside, and store the envelopes in one of your boxes. And of course, baskets are perfect for storing arts and crafts for the kids, sewing materials, even gift ribbon and bows. Over the years people have said to me, "You're so organized!" I believe a few friends think I take it too far, but my systems make my life work more smoothly. We each have to find our own style for life management. When you do find your own system, you can live more abundantly for other purposes! Why waste precious time?

GO *for the* GOAL

Where are you headed? Your answer to that question is a key to your future! If you find yourself in a constant panic, a lot of time may be wasted because you don't know where you're going. It's important to set goals. But doing so doesn't just happen. Set your large goals and break them into smaller ones. Where do you want to be in five years? What about three? One year? Six months? The progression is important! How you plan today will tell you where you're headed. Sure, you can fill your time with activities; that's easy. But by goal setting, everything you do can be directed toward a purpose—one that's aligned with God's will for your life!

PAPER WEIGHT LIFTED

With all the laptops, PDAs, and computer gizmos, why are we still buried in paper? A few tips that help me may be just what you need. First, I consider junk mail a time waster; it gets tossed. If I don't have time to read publications, missionary letters, magazines, I put them in a file folder and take them with me as I run my errands. You can read mail when your car's being washed or you're waiting at the doctor's office. If it's an invitation, make a note on your calendar, respond with a call, and then toss it! Paper is always going to be a part of life. We can't make it disappear—but we can manage it! A little organization can relieve a lot of stress!

SNIFF *and* SMILE

If you decide to "take time to smell the roses," how do you put it into practice? Practice saying no until you can clearly think through the new responsibility of time and effort being asked of you. Time is precious, so focus on what's really important to God for your life. Find pleasure in fewer possessions. Just about everything you bring into your home is going to require repairing and maintenance. Look at your budget. Do you spend more money than you have? If you're feeling overwhelmed, recharge your battery—take a time out! Find a hobby you enjoy. Someone once said it doesn't matter what it is—as long as it makes you smile. A simpler life is possible. It begins with a daily commitment to do less—not more!

STRESS BE GONE

Organized! If just the word makes you cringe—then read on! It might surprise you to know that 85 percent of your stress is caused by—*disorganization*. Why do you think all these new organization-type cable shows are so popular? The benefits to having order in your life are so worth it—stress relieved, hours redeemed, goals achieved. And the result is a new, fresh joy. You know that I am all about simplifying life. That means getting rid of "stuff" you don't use. A friend of mine confessed to filling four giant plastic bags with nothing but clothes she no longer wears! The bottom line is having less stress and more energy. Learn to take the simple way for day-to-day living so that when trials appear, you are better prepared and a lot less frantic or worried.

COMMIT *to* COMMITMENT

We seem to like to "wing it" in life today. We like to remain in contact with lots of people, and we enjoy the benefits of technology, but we also fly by the seat of our pants even with all this networking and information available. Why? Because we don't like the idea of commitment of any kind. Commitment can be perceived as restriction and limitation, but if we commit to life-giving things, we actually have more freedom and opportunity. Planning can sound boring and so much like commitment that people run the opposite direction toward willy-nilly living. Planning can open up your life in ways you cannot imagine until you implement a touch of it in your life. Once you do, you will see that committing to people, goals, and a bit of structure gives you a great foundation.

PERSONAL *and* PRACTICAL

Shall we get really practical? If you're anything like me, you may be a bit challenged when it comes to electrical things. If so, color code your extension cords when you have several at one outlet. Sew extra buttons for your clothing on the inside or at the bottom of an item. No looking around for just the right button when you need it! Tape the extra screws that come with furniture to the underside of chairs, sofas, and tables. And always refill that gas tank *before* it's on empty! Take inventory of your pantry or primary kitchen food cupboards and see what items seem to never get used and which ones are always being restocked. Keep this information in mind, or better yet on a list, so that you can streamline your next trip to the grocery store. I told you we were going for practical!

SALE TIME

Experts say that the fastest-selling garage-sale items are usually furniture. Chests of drawers in particular, followed by dish sets and flower arrangements, believe it or not! Other garage-sale favorites are baby items and electronic equipment. Sporting goods always sell big as well. One surefire idea is to have a prominently displayed bargain bin with anything you want to sell quickly. The whole idea is to get rid of some of the junk (oops—I mean wonderful quality items!)

you have lying around. It is also wonderful to provide items of need to those in need. Don't forget to take care of your used items so that you can either sell them at a deal or give them to nonprofits.

SHARE, STORE, *or* KEEP

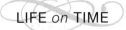

When space is at a premium—that's when you have to work smart! Here are some ideas that work for me. Remodel that antique armoire and put your entertainment center inside. Use boxes—you've certainly heard me say that before—because they make great storage containers. You can stack them just about anywhere. Use the tops of cabinets and hutches to creatively store flower arrangements—or any attractive item. Luggage you're not using—ideal storage. Oh, by the way, throwing out or giving away things you no longer use also works! Above all, we need to evaluate what we "store" and "keep." The Bible says where your treasure is reveals the values of your heart!

LIFE *on* TIME

Some women are always late for appointments. Of course, I'm not talking about you! It's frustrating if you're the one who's waiting—friend or not! Maybe it's a bit devious, but some people beg to be given a different starting time by their past record. If you want to meet for lunch, make it for a half-hour earlier than you need to be there. If it's your children who are always slow to get out the door, set the alarm to go off five minutes before it's time for them to head out the door. Call it an early-warning system. Who knows! It might even work. Frankly, I want time and a joyous spirit for the really important things God has for me to do. When we are always running late, behind, and frantic, it takes us out of the joy of each moment and activity. It also ruins our mood for the rest of the day! Stay up on the time and up in spirit.

WHEN ORDER IS *in the* WAY

Luke 10 tells the story about two sisters: Mary and Martha. Martha becomes upset because she has done so much work to prepare for Jesus' visit while Mary has neglected the chores to spend time with their guest. Jesus tells Martha, "Mary has chosen the good part, which shall not be taken away from her" (verse 42). I so want to be like Mary—but Martha gets in the way. She wants to clean and have everything in order before guests arrive. I'm sure Martha mopped and cleaned all day before Jesus arrived. But Mary understood that Jesus was more important, that the preparation needed to take place in her *heart*. My prayer is that you and I will have a passion for Jesus. That we will learn to say no to even good things to make room for the very best things for our lives and the lives of our family members, friends, and neighbors. Don't settle for hurried activities when there is a chance for meaningful matters to emerge.

DITCH *the* CAPE

With just a few changes, life can be a lot less hectic! My prayer for you today is that you'll give up trying to be superwoman. Super mom, super wife, super everything! It's very tiring—and lonely. And it leads to burnout and certainly disappointment. You need a little teamwork at your house. Your husband and your children should be helping you manage all that has to be done. And you need to let them! The result can be rich blessings—of self-respect, pride for a job well done, and a feeling of cooperation. You'll notice the whole family's attitude will change. And you can give up being superwoman! At *last!*

AN ORDER *for* ORDER

Bring order out of confusion! God delights in turning our weaknesses into strengths. And did you know that God redeems our time and our tasks? When our "house is in order"—communication is better, we're able to do problem solving, things get done, and relationships are better. Organization begins with you. And remember the reward. It's more time to do God's will in your life. Here's a thought for you to hide in your heart today: People before things. People before projects. Family before friends. Husband before children. Giving before wants. And God's Word before opinions. Jesus before all.

EASY SOLUTIONS

I'm here to interrupt you—just for a minute! Bob used to always waste time looking for the car keys and his glasses. One day I put up a key hook by the phone in the kitchen and told him to put his car keys on the hook and his glasses on the counter underneath. Done deal—no more problem. Reduce some of that early-morning stress by getting things ready the night before. Sounds simple enough. Yet most people run around in the morning, trying to find their briefcases, packing lunches—whatever. Lists are a lifesaver. And here's a bonus tip for today: Take control of your time. You need as much time as you can get for the really important things you want to do.

IN-BETWEEN BONUS

Use what I call in-between times to get things done. For example, it only takes 15 minutes to change the sheets. Use one of those in-between times to get it done. The importance of planning is that it saves you time in the end. Know what you have to do—and set your priorities. Get rid of paper. Almost 90 percent of the paper in your home or office is never used. Break projects into small jobs and complete the little pieces. Write down your goals. The success rate is so much greater when you do. Set a schedule. Eliminate interruptions.

Be positive about being organized. And here's a little bonus tip for today: Total organization doesn't exist. It's a lifetime process. So relax and remember to keep it simple.

NEST *for* REST

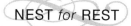

To me, it's hard to feel comfortable in a house that's dirty, cluttered, or disorganized. Oh, I know—we're all different in what we can tolerate. But I'm convinced that some sense of organization and order are absolutely necessary for most people to feel—at home! Create a comfortable nest where people you love, including yourself, can work and play and relax and visit. The point of it all, of course, is making yourself and other people feel at home. Here's a little bonus tip for today: Make yourself comfortable—and create a comfortable place for others. Chances are that the same colors, furniture arrangements, and lighting that gives you rest and peace will also extend the same gifts to your visitors.

GIFT CLOSETS

Take an hour or so at a store and load up on all kinds of greeting cards—birthday, anniversary, "just because" cards, etc. Then go home and file them away. You'll save a lot of time and aggravation later on. Here's another tip: Have a gift shelf in your home. Load it up with little boxes of stationery, stuffed toys—whatever is useful and on sale. When grandchildren drop by, let them pick a little gift off your shelf. I also love my gift-wrap shelf—complete with all the supplies I need. What a lifesaver! And here's a little bonus tip for you: Your time is valuable. Preserve mental and physical energy, not to mention some gas, by cutting back on the small errands that eat away at your days. The above ideas allow you to breathe easier when special events and occasions arise.

Keeping It Simple

BIG IDEAS, SMALL SPACES

If you're running out of space—keep reading! I have a friend who lives in a small beach apartment—and believe me, there's absolutely no wasted space. Install a towel rack on the inside of a closet door to hang tablecloths. Her armoire stores her DVD, CD player, radio—all kinds of things. And on the top she keeps her baskets— very decoratively I might add. Boxes are great storage places. Cover them in bright colors to match your rooms and store away! Use the top of everything—refrigerator, cabinets, hutches—just make it look decorative and you've got great storage areas. And here's a bonus tip for today: You know that luggage you have sitting around? You're tracking with me! Fill them right up with items you need to store.

MEMORY TRIGGERS

Getting organized seems to be everyone's concern. It's simple once you put your mind to it. It starts with you. Do you have a plan? If you don't, you need one. Write everything down. Don't rely on your memory. Keep a little notebook with you, jot down things that come to mind or things you need to do. Once you write it down, don't forget to read it later! Don't laugh. That's where a lot of us miss it! And by all means, keep lists, lists, lists. Believe me, it won't take long before you feel a lot more organized. Then you can go on to the bigger stuff.

SPONTANEOUS PLANNING!

There's good reason to stay on top of things! Allow spontaneity in your life. It helps. As crazy as it sounds, spontaneity requires a lot of careful planning. Ironic isn't it? But that's one reason I encourage you to organize your life—to keep on top of that housework. Have a centerpiece you can pull out for last-minute occasions. Keep silk flowers on hand and a supply of candles. Cook ahead. Have backups in the freezer—spaghetti sauce, a tamale-pie casserole, frozen piecrust—whatever. When you do, you're always ready for a quick tea party or dinner with old friends—or new ones! When you plan for spontaneous hospitality, it's such a gift. Here's the bonus tip for today: Friendships happen through spending time together. *Purposely* plan to make that happen!

REMINISCE *and* PASS ALONG

Why not take a day and dig through those storage boxes, flip through the photo albums, pull out those baby clothes packed away long ago, sift through recipes stashed in your kitchen drawers, really look at the loose family photos at the back of the family Bible. As you go through simple items that you've had around awhile, you will reminisce about good times tied to each item. It is always good to reconnect with the things that bring you joy—a delicate cut-glass vase, a child's drawing, a grandfather's old letters. These are some of the things that make up your heritage. Enjoy them. But also pass the stories—and the treasures—along to your children and your grandchildren. Give them a sense of the past and the anticipation of their future as a member of your family—and as a member of God's family!

KITCHEN TIPS

If half-folded grocery bags are falling out all over the place every time you open the pantry or cupboard door, read on! If you want to keep everything in the right place—label your shelves. It's so much easier to find things in a hurry. Store as much as possible in plastic containers or jars—everything from tea bags to flour and noodles to coffee filters. They'll stay fresher much longer, and you can see what is in them at a glance. Save one of your larger shelves for appliances—group them according to function. The same thing applies to your freezer and any other storage areas. You'll be surprised at how a little organization will save you precious time and stress.

FRIDGE REPAIR

Go ahead, I dare you. Open your refrigerator door. Kind of intimidating, isn't it? Who knows how long *that* container has been in there! Your refrigerator is just another closet, so let's get organized! Your best friends are plastic containers and bags. Lazy Susans are great space savers. Use them to hold sour cream, cottage cheese, jellies, peanut butter—and whatever else is cluttering up your refrigerator. Be sure to avoid "mystery packages" in your freezer. Here's a tip: Shape hamburger into patties, freeze on a cookie sheet, and then transfer to plastic bags. They won't stick together and they're ready to use. You'll love opening your refrigerator after applying all these tips.

CAR CONTAINER

That car of yours has a gem of a storage space! What, haven't you noticed? It's your *glove compartment*. Are you shocked? Whoever heard of organizing the glove compartment? Laugh if you will—but believe me, this checklist will help in all kinds of stressful situations. Here we go: maps, notepad and pen, tire-pressure gauge, clean-up wipes, sunglasses, reading material, a travel Bible—you can enjoy reading during waiting times in the car. Other items to have in your handy vehicle storage space include plastic forks and spoons, change for parking, business cards, Band-Aids, note cards, scissors, nail clippers, and more. It helps if you have an extra large glove compartment! The idea is to be prepared. As I said, it's a simple way to avoid a lot of frustration!

TRIP MAKERS

Do you have a trip coming up? Here are a few simple tips for avoiding jet lag! A friend of mine just returned from South Africa. That's 30 hours of travel and a lot of jet lag. Yet she arrived and headed out for a full day of sightseeing and felt great. Here's her advice: Three days before, start eliminating sugar from your diet. And keep those caffeinated drinks to a minimum. On each leg of the trip, reset your watch to your destination time. During the flight and the day of arrival, don't oversleep. Don't drink caffeine, avoid napping, and go to sleep at 10:00 P.M. or so—destination time. And throughout the flight drink a lot of water. Sleep and eat on your destination time schedule. It makes travel less stressful and more restful.

STORAGE SOLUTIONS

I don't know about you—but I never have enough storage space. Armoires and other large storage pieces were invented when walk-in closets were unheard of. They're still a great buy, but a less expensive alternative is a rolling clothes rack. Just hide it behind a folding screen, or use a curtain to transform the entire end of a room into a closet and dressing area. Roomy trunks or cedar chests are also great storage places. Another interesting way to meet your bedroom storage needs is to place beautiful items in plain view. Hang your hats on the wall, drape chains and necklaces from a series of decorative hooks. A peg rail is simple and works great for hanging all kinds of clothing items. Why hide some of your most decorative belongings?

CONFINED CHAOS

You might want to try some controlled chaos mixed with some soft lighting and a few quiet moments! Sound too good to be true? Frankly, I have to have my chaos controlled! I've never liked mass confusion with everyone running around like chickens with their heads cut off. When I was younger, I was a complete wreck because of the stress of the family. It was only when I learned to be proactive that things turned around. I understood that organization wasn't something just for other people or people with money. Organization was my key to making life work. That's why I spend so much time talking about organization and keeping life simple. Ask God to show you the balance you need—make your home a place for some stillness. Turn off the TV, play some soft music instead. Smell the roses!

LET IT OVERFLOW

Count on it! From time to time—your teacup is going to overflow! "After you have suffered for a little while, the God of all grace...will Himself perfect, confirm, strengthen and establish you" (1 Peter

5:10). There are going to be some dark shadows. But even at those times, your cup will overflow with God's goodness and mercy. How do I know? I've been there. I've experienced God's grace in the midst of the worst four years of my life battling cancer. And now, when the clouds are lifting, I see so much more clearly. I see how I've been restored and strengthened. It didn't happen exactly the way I thought it would. But you know? The results were so much deeper—and more wonderful—than I could imagine.

CHEER UP CHORES

Getting children to help around the house isn't as simple as it sounds! I think most moms envision one day their children being old enough to jump in and help. They might, but unless they are trained up in basic responsibilities, you won't stand a chance of this happening. I have a few tips that worked for me. If you want your children to grow up believing the mess belongs to the person who made it, then don't teach them they're helping mommy. Instead, applaud them for making *their* bed, dressing *themselves,* and putting *their* clothes away. From an early age, teach your children to be responsible for their own clothes, bed, laundry, and toys. Make the chores fun and games. A preschooler can set the table. Young children can take out the trash. Simple chores. The idea is that children can learn to love to do their fair share around the house!

START *with* HOPE

This is the day the Lord has made! Let's rejoice and be glad in it! I can't think of a better way to start the day. When you begin in a "frenzied flurry," that's pretty much the way it'll go all day! Been there, done that! Instead, make your mornings hopeful and hope filled. You heard me correctly. Be hopeful. I have a slightly radical idea for those busy days. Put on your favorite snuggly bathrobe, enjoy a quiet cup of coffee or tea, and add a little music in the background. Open your Bible to a favorite passage—then ask God for the strength—and courage—to spend that day in hope! Give the day clarity and meaning. Hold every moment sacred!

TRAVEL LIGHT

When you are traveling, don't take more luggage to the airport than you can carry yourself! If you can't carry it—you're taking too much. And clean out your purse or tote bag. There's at least a pound of stuff in there—receipts you don't need, ticket stubs, loose change. Be sure you have some kind of expandable tote bag. You might as well count on having a place for all the souvenirs and gifts you plan to buy. Pack normally. Then take out half the clothes. Yep—half! And all those shoes? I don't think so! Lightening up every day is a great way to travel through your life journey too.

PERMISSION

Often it's just some little tip that makes all the difference. If you're feeling guilty about all that needs to be done around the house—let it go! If you can't give yourself permission to let some things slide for a while, then I will. Let it go. There's always going to be some kind of mess to clean up. If you've got a hectic schedule, break up the tasks into time slots and then stick to those time slots. Plan menus two weeks at a time and shop for everything at once. And by all means, lower your expectations. There's a big difference between dirty and messy. Save time for the really important moments in life!

STEP *by* STEP

There's an old story about a clock that began to think how many times during the year ahead it would have to tick: 31,536,000 seconds in *one year!* The clock just got tired at the thought and said, "I can't do it." When the clock was reminded it didn't have to tick the seconds all at one time—but one by one—it began to run again and everything was all right. When I'm able to break up my day into small pieces, I'm much less overwhelmed by everything I need to do. I can even laugh along the way! I guess what I'm trying to say is: A long journey begins with the *first* step!

HOME HOMEWORK

It's time for a quiz! Give yourself one point for every yes. Do you have enough space? Are things piling up in the closet? Are there stacks of unread magazines sitting around? Do certain items constantly get lost? Are things collecting on the top of your refrigerator? Are you finding stuff you haven't used in over a year! Are you buying things you already have—because you can't find them? If you score 0–3: pretty good! 4–6 means you could definitely use some improvement! Set aside one hour this week to think through solutions for any of these problem areas that you recognized as a big factor in your life. This is your official homework. Try preserving that one hour a week for the next month.

PROJECT FRIENDSHIP

Here are a few tips for quality time with that friend you rarely get to see. One idea I heard about involves cleaning out closets. Before you groan too loudly—there's more to this. They organized three baskets. One for charity, one for trash, and one for items that go back into the closets—and they had a lot of fun doing it together. Another good friend project is to dump all those photos you've both accumulated on your kitchen table. Start organizing them for family memory books or to create CDs with your favorite photos. It's a great time for talking about your kids, your marriages—and best of all—your walk with the Lord. Maybe it's time you started your own Project Friendship!

STEP ONE

Take your day—one step at a time! On those days when you'd rather not face the mountain of tasks ahead, just put your feet on the floor and take that first step of the day. When I'm able to break up a large day into small pieces, it's not nearly as overwhelming. And you know what? I usually manage to get everything done—and sometimes I can even laugh along the way. Tomorrow when you wake up—what's the first thing you need to do? Do it! What's the second thing? Do it. Take your day one step at a time. And thank God for each new beginning!

FAMILY PLAN

"Do the worst first!" Here's a simple battle plan for cleaning up the messes! In many homes that means the garage, closets, kitchen cupboards—or just general paper messes. Okay, here are a few tips as you're planning your attack. Turn on some upbeat music. No telephone calls. No visitors unless they're helping you. Have everyone help on the big projects. Concentrate on one project or area at a time And remember, some things have to go—fill that trash can! No TV or any other distractions. Set a date on your calendar so you can attack these monster projects as a team. "United we stand, divided we fall" kind of thing. Bribe the family with a special trip, food, or luxury item. Believe me, it's worth it! And here's another tip. Try to make it fun!

The Organized Life

SELF-ORGANIZATION

After I finished a seminar on how to organize a household, a young mother rushed forward to tell me, "I loved all the organizational ideas and tips you gave for the family and home. But what about *me?* How do *I* get organized?" I pulled my daily planner out of my purse. This is a tool I've used for years to get me through each day, week, month, and year of my life. I'd be lost without it. Organization really starts with our personal daily lives. Once we've organized ourselves, we can move more confidently into the other areas of our lives—such as family, home, or job. Get organized and make life a whole lot simpler.

SECRETS *to* MY SUCCESS

Women always ask me how to be more organized. Well, there are four basic tools you've got to have: (1) a monthly calendar—at-a-glance; at one look you can see the days, dates, holidays; (2) a daily schedule that has 15-minute blocks of time for scheduling the activities of the day; remember not to overcrowd your schedule—you'll just be frustrated; (3) have a telephone/address book and include all the numbers you need to have for your daily activities; (4) and you'll need some kind of filing system. Time can be your friend if you learn how to make it work for you. It's been my observation over many years that successful people know how to use their allotted time as a friend—not as a time waster.

HOME AWAY *from* HOME

How about some simple ways to make life more enjoyable? When you take that vacation, take along a clock radio, family pictures, or a prayer basket with Bible and a prayer organizer to help you create a welcoming home away from home. Or sometime during an evening at home, turn down the sheets. Borrow an idea from fine hotels and leave a chocolate or a little sachet on the pillow. Something as simple as parsley in a jar of water in the refrigerator looks inviting when you open it. I also enjoy keeping a bouquet of parsley on the windowsill by the sink. I know these little things sometimes seem trivial—but you know what? Life is hectic enough, and a little gentleness, a little creativity, help make you feel pampered whether you are on the road or nestled in your favorite room at home.

CHOOSE CONTENTMENT

When you're overwhelmed, you can't see new opportunities, challenges—or even how to care for another person. It's like, "Are you kidding? I've got too much to handle already!" Establish goals for your life. It's basic! If you want to eliminate mess and clutter from your life—ask yourself these questions: Who am I? Where am I going? What do I need to get there? Will this save me money? Will that save me time? Does this improve the quality of my life? You can choose to be content. But as long as you choose "dis-content"—you'll have clutter in your personal affairs. These basics are lifetime pursuits in growing into the woman that God wants you to become.

DREAM *a* LITTLE

It's a kid's dream—banana splits for dinner! Go ahead, Mom—just once turn dinner into a celebration by serving sundaes or banana splits. Yes, for your main meal! It's a lot less fattening than dinner plus banana splits, and once won't ruin anyone's health. How does this relate to organization? It is good to plan for fun. Sometimes it just rises up in a moment. But other times we go about our days very locked in to routine and rules and schedules. Plan to surprise your family with simple joys that give a lift to their spirits and also serve to reconnect you with each of them. Nothing unites a family better than shared smiles. A lot of conversation will be sparked as well. Don't forget everyone's favorite toppings!

ROOM *to* GO DEEPER

Clutter wearies the spirit and fights against serenity. At the very least, take 15 minutes to dejunk the room where you spend your quiet time. Keep a Bible, writing paper, and a pen on your bedside table for spiritual food during still moments. Read Ecclesiastes 3—the whole chapter. Then make a list of where you are in *your* life right now. What percentage of your life is available for inward pursuits? How often do we spend time assessing our hearts and our dreams? Not often enough! Let this be a time to get to know yourself better and also get to know your Creator better.

MONEY MATTERS

Make it a point to organize all those financial records you've got sitting in drawers and closets. Good financial records can often equal good decisions! Here's a seven-step plan: (1) know what to keep; separate permanent records from current records; (2) use a system that works for you; (3) set aside a spot for your records; something fireproof is best and permanent documents should be kept in a safe-deposit box; (4) tell someone where your records are; (5) get professional advice on handling records, especially when it comes to taxes; (6) revamp your system when you make a life change; (7) set aside time for record keeping. If you're untrustworthy about worldly wealth, who will trust you with the true riches of heaven? Hey, I didn't say it—the Bible did!

IN-HOUSE CEO

This may be the year that God will bring into your life the desire to be an at-home woman—and develop a from-home business. It *is* possible! In fact, that's how my husband and I started our ministry, More Hours in My Day. One woman I read about shops for working women. Another creative mom does gift wrapping for people in offices. Another mom advertised her famous chili recipe for one dollar. She sold enough to buy Christmas presents for the whole family. I visited friends who received an adorable loaf of bread, shaped like a teddy bear. This novelty gift is now being shipped all over the state. My desire is to see the busy woman get back to traditional values—to use her God-given creativity wherever she may be—in or out of the home.

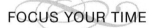

FOCUS YOUR TIME

Time can be your friend if you learn how to make it work for you. Many of us waste time because we don't have clear direction for our lives. Have you ever sat down and wrote out your life purpose? It might surprise you in what you discover. It's hard to choose good use of our time if we're not sure what we want to do with it. I have a friend who decided when she turned 50 that she wanted to devote her personal time primarily to the interests of abused children. Because of her goal, decisions about how to use her time became quite simple. Successful people know how to use their allotted time as a friend—not as a time waster. You can start today—it's that simple!

YOU CAN LEARN

Look around you! Being neat doesn't always mean being organized! It's not "Where do I put it?" It's "Where do I *find* it?" There's a big difference. When your office (or your life for that matter) is too messy, you can't utilize your time wisely. You spend more time trying to find things than doing anything about the project at hand. What's the clutter costing you? Most likely time, money, and, if you're operating a business, customers! And what's the message you're passing along to your family? Remember, being organized is not a personality trait. It's a skill you can learn. The secret is getting organized and maintaining it over the long haul. Once you've accomplished that, you're ready to meet the challenges of each new day with renewed energy.

FIVE-MINUTE FILE

The average person wastes two and a half hours every day. If we could have those hours free all in a single block of time, wouldn't that be great? But in five- or ten-minute segments you can get a lot done. The key is to use the five-minute segments to accomplish a small task or make a dent in a large one. File your nails, make appointments, clean a shelf, throw in a load of laundry, write a note to someone you thought of this week. One pastor provided a copy of the Psalms for everyone in his congregation. He suggests they use it when they have a minute or so of free time or "waiting time" as he calls it. Make your own five-minute file of ideas, articles, and to-do possibilities. You'll be amazed at what you can accomplish in these increments. It also breathes more patience into those waiting times.

SPACE *for* GRACE

Could you watch television 25 percent less? Could you get up just 15 minutes earlier? With creativity and God's help you can make time and some space for your relationship with Him and add more to your life. Maybe the most obvious way is to schedule in your quiet time. Why not? There are some things that can only be accomplished as we meet with the Lord in quiet. First Thessalonians 4:11-12 says, "Make it your ambition to lead a quiet life, to mind your own business and to work with your hands, just as we told you, so that your daily life may win the respect of outsiders and so that you will not be dependent on anybody" (NIV). A rich quiet time helps you discover God as your sole source of life, strength, and hope.

PANTRY *of the* HEART

I want to encourage you today to stock your pantry with a knowledge of the Father, the Son, and the Holy Spirit. For long periods during my difficult and painful cancer years my eyes wouldn't focus and I couldn't read. Yet there were so many sleepless nights when Scripture came flooding back to me from years before. So many afternoons—barely awake from medication—the Psalms Bob read me sifted through the haze. Years of prayer. Years of trusting God. Years of getting to know Him on an intimate level. And even my "15 Minutes a Day" organization habit prompted me to pray when I didn't think I had time, or energy, or the will to do it. I say all of this simply to encourage you to fill that pantry of yours with God, with His grace, and with His faithfulness.

ON TARGET

If you don't have a target—you'll never know if you have a hit or a miss! We all need a few simple tips for making life work. Goal setting doesn't just happen. We have to take time to think long range if we're going to have an effective plan. Those ten-year goals have to be portioned into smaller goals so that tomorrow you know how to proceed. Sure, we can fill our time with activities; that's easy. But goal setting directs us toward a purpose. If my goal for this summer is to read five books—then what book will I read first? If I want to memorize more Scripture—where will I begin tomorrow? Don't be afraid to set your sights on a target. Our goals become road maps for our lives, but they are not cast in concrete; they are flexible and ever changing.

RECIPE *for* SUCCESS

For those of us who are most at home in the kitchen, think of organization as a recipe for success. Here are some of the ingredients you'll need: 1 quality period of time with God each day, 1 list of carefully thought through long-term and short-term goals, 1 list of priority activities to get you to your goals, 1 monthly calendar, 1 weekly schedule book, 1 pad of daily schedules, and 1 good time-management book. Mix the ingredients liberally and season them with prayer. Blend them into your life. The result will be an organized home and a happier woman! Are you ready to begin? Don't delay a moment longer in working toward a more organized you.

ORGANIZATION'S CORNERSTONE

If I had to choose one organizational ingredient as the most essential, it would be my daily planner. It almost never leaves my side! I even keep a larger version at home. My home instruction page is a weekly routine of chores and errands. A quick glance is all I need. Another section is for important numbers—everything from ambulance to veterinarian to neighbors. Credit cards are listed in another section. You get the idea. One last tip. The larger notebook isn't always convenient, so I keep a daily reminder pad in my kitchen. Three columns on bright yellow paper: "Call," "Do," and "See." Just take an hour or so to invest in your daily planner. You'll redeem that hour in one day, I guarantee it!

FIVE PIECES *to* PEACE

Today let's determine we're going to throw away anything we don't need! Those recipes, articles, school papers, old magazines, and receipts. Choose five pieces and toss the rest into your trash bag. Actually start with whatever clutter annoys you the most. If you're one of those people who never throws anything away—you may be experiencing a bit of anxiety at the moment! But life can be so much simpler. Go through those drawers and closets where paper has accumulated—and just start tossing. The other day I found old receipts from clothing I'd purchased two years ago. Out they went! Here's another helpful hint: Develop a simple yet thorough file system and stick to it! When our lives are cluttered—often our hearts are cluttered—there's no room left over for the important things. Clear the way by starting with five pieces.

HIDE IT *in* STYLE

Stuff! Quite simply—we have too much of it! Stuff fills our lives. We don't know where to put it. We don't know how to hide it. Or we don't know how to use it. Here are a few all-purpose strategies that work. Use a decorated screen. It will cover a magnitude of decorating sins! Actually, it's a beautiful decorating piece on its own. Paint it, texture it, antique it—be creative. Furniture can sometimes serve the same purpose. An armoire placed at an angle across a corner creates a beautiful, perfect storage nook for little-used items. A bookcase standing out from the wall gives you an instant storage space. Get your creative mind going—you'll be surprised at what you come up with.

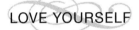

LOVE YOURSELF

"If I could only have a better nose, a tuck here and there, blond hair…if I could only be more like so-and-so, I would be okay as a person." I'm simply urging you to dump those negative thoughts. It can poison your system. We can't be lifted up when we spend so much time tearing ourselves down. God didn't make a mistake when He created you. Have you ever realized that God made you uniquely different from everyone else? Yes, it's important to work on improving imperfections, but don't dwell on them so much that you forget who you are in the sight of God. Go easy on yourself. Here's a simple fact to remember: the way we'll improve our self-image is by being positive and acknowledging that we are God's creation. When we do this, we won't use up so much of our time and energy on trying to change who we are.

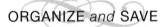

ORGANIZE *and* SAVE

The best way to save money when you hit the supermarket is to plan ahead. Check your local newspaper ads for sales. If something is on sale, buy in quantity. Generic brands can be a savings. By all means avoid impulse buying. Studies estimate that nearly 50 percent of all purchases are unplanned. Good for the store—bad for you!

Complete your shopping in half an hour. It's those extra minutes that bring on the impulse buying. "Who cares?" Well, for one, I do! You know why? Because it gives me more hours in my day—and more money in my pocket—to do those things that count the most! Is life about being a great shopper? No, it's about being the woman God desires you to be, and that takes some leisure time.

$\mathcal{A}$ Peaceful Place

PITCH IN

You want a few simple tips for getting children to help out around the house? Okay, we're dreaming here! But it is amazing how plastic bins, pegs, hampers, baskets, and hooks give your children resources to pick up and put away their things. Teach them to pitch in, and show them how it helps the entire family. Here's an idea for young children when they want a straw for their drink. Cut it off short so it's easier to hold and drink from. Put a laundry basket in each child's room. Have them help sort clothes on laundry day. Another important tip: Catch your child doing something good and tell him or her about it. Be positive and uplifting. And when all else fails, get a friend to come over and give you a break. You deserve it.

FRIENDS HELPING FRIENDS

I was staying in the home of a couple that was moving in two days. As I looked around, nothing was packed. I finally asked about it. "Oh, no," she explained, "I don't pack at all. On moving day there will be 20 to 30 men from the church. They'll pack and move the entire household to our new 'old' home where the women are scrubbing, painting, and wallpapering. By dinnertime, food will be brought in for everyone." Friends helping friends. This same group told me that when a woman became pregnant, ten ladies—in one afternoon—sewed an entire maternity wardrobe for her to wear and enjoy. I was absolutely overwhelmed. Ralph Waldo Emerson said, "Friendship, like the immortality of the soul, is too good to be believed."

WORRY-FREE LIFE

Matthew 6:25 says, "Do not worry about your life" (NIV). How true and yet how simple a thought that is. As I've observed my five grandchildren over the years, one thing stands out vividly—their ability to live and enjoy the moment. As I get older, I'm trying to forget about what happened yesterday—and what might happen tomorrow—and just experience the fullness of today. How about you? So often, our anxieties are about situations we have no control over. Eighty-five percent of the things we worry about never happen. Let's read the rest of Matthew 6:25: "...what you will eat or drink; or about your body, what you will wear. Is not life more important than food, and the body more important than clothes?" God cares about every detail. May today be the greatest day of your life!

SAY NO—EVEN *to* YOURSELF

Do you want more time for yourself and your family? Of course you do—but how? First of all, make a to-do list, and be sure to set some manageable deadlines. Use a brief time for bite-sized tasks, like writing a note, cleaning a bathroom, or changing the bed. And be sure to watch out for interruptions. Use your answering machine.

Or let calls go to your voice mail if you are in the middle of something. Learn to say no until you've completed what you've set out to do. Sometimes this involves saying no to yourself. We can be our worst distracter! And by all means, get your family to help you. And be sure you reward yourself. Have lunch with a friend or sit down with a cup of tea.

FACE IT

If you're a procrastinator, getting into motion can be frustrating! Do you need a push? Maybe these hints will help you get started. Face the tasks you have to do right in the eye. Ignoring them doesn't make them go away. Make a commitment to someone—then ask a friend to hold you accountable for getting started. Here's the one I like best: Give yourself a reward. And by all means, give yourself deadlines. Color code the due date on your calendar if you have to. And be decisive. Have the courage to act. Don't be crippled by the "what ifs," the "I'm gonnas," and the "I wants"—make something happen!

GOD'S ORDER

If you are anything like me, you respond positively to order in your life. I believe it's because we're made in the image of God—and because God organized the whole universe to go forward in an orderly fashion. He's the ultimate organizer! And the results of His ordering Spirit are always good. Unless you begin with the heart, the most complete reorganization of house and home will just drive you crazy. As we open our hearts and attitudes to God, putting Him first in our lives, He will show us little ways to organize the chaos—and lead a more peaceful, ordered existence. It takes time—be patient. Growing in the Spirit is a lifelong process!

THE INVITING HOME

When your home has a logical arrangement, it becomes more inviting for all who live or visit there. Once the door is open, the basics should be in order—a place to wipe feet, a place to hang coats. The entranceway sets the mood and sends a message about the whole house. A neat foyer with a shiny floor and sparkling mirror says, "This house is orderly and peaceful." A cozy apartment living room with plump cushions, soft music, and lots of candles says, "Come on in—let's get to know you." And of course the smell of something wonderful on the stove is an unmistakable welcome. I know of more than one person who's sold her house quickly by popping a loaf of bread dough into the oven before prospective buyers showed up. Simple—but inviting!

SIMPLE *and* CLASSIC

Baskets! By now I'm probably known as the "basket lady." But they're an inexpensive and beautiful solution to all sorts of storage problems. If you have no place for a desk, fill a storage box with office supplies—store it in a closet or under a bed. A piece of plywood on two sawhorses makes a wonderful space for cutting out clothes or doing craft projects. Use bookcases to hold children's toys, sewing equipment—even office supplies. Paint your file cabinets to match your rooms—or hide them under a skirted table. Arrange hats or scarves on hooks on a wall. There's so much you can do that is both creative and—what's the magic word? Simple!

FALL *into* ORDER

When your children head back to school is a great opportunity to get organized for the academic year. This year let's plan ahead and make it a whole lot simpler than last year. You can start in the closet. A lot of summer clothing can be stored away for next summer. Put them in boxes and label the boxes according to size. Then next year, they can be passed along to other family members or friends. Always cycle those perfectly good clothes. Make up a checklist now for what you'll need this fall. Even have your children help with an inventory list—shoes, socks, T-shirts, pants, uniforms if you use them. Get everything ready now and avoid the rush later. Now comes the fun part! Shopping for school. By planning ahead, you can make it a special time for you and your children.

JAZZ UP YOUR CLEANING

There's no question—housework is a nuisance! Be sure to use what I call the Speedy Easy Method. You'll love it. Put on some music with a very fast beat. Make it fun by moving to the music as you clean. You'll get a workout, and the cleaning will go faster—and take your mind off the drudgery. Here's a tip: Use your hair dryer to blow off the dust from silk flowers. Or after wiping clean your wastebaskets, give the inside bottom a coat of floor wax. It will prevent trash from sticking to the bottom. Having proper tools sure helps. And don't feel everything has to be done in one session. And then, of course, there's the Emilie Rule! Reward yourself! And when you're finished, pick some flowers for your beautiful, clean house!

PACK-RAT TOUR

Are things collecting on top of your refrigerator, counters, end tables, and bookshelves? Do you often say, "It might come in handy—someday"? You may be a classic pack rat. Or it could be that you just don't realize how many odds and ends you tuck away in these places. Walk through your house and take an inventory of these hiding places for your collecting habit. Then take another tour, but this time walk through with boxes or a large garbage bag. Gather these rarely used or thought of items, place them in the box or bag, and then place them out in the garage. If they sit for several months untouched—it's a sure signal to give them away or throw them away. If you're going to be a pack rat—at least be an organized one!

THINK MULTIPURPOSE

One of my favorite pieces of furniture is an odd little cabinet I bought for $15 at a garage sale. It's long and low—with doors in front. We use it as a table behind our sofa, with a little lamp and an antique scale on top. It's also wonderful for storing tablecloths and napkins. Whenever we're in an antique store, we're on the lookout for multipurpose pieces. Over the years, we've collected an oak icebox that stores our crystal, a Hoosier cabinet that proudly displays teapots and teacups—and a variety of wardrobes and bookcases that offer storage. They all look so beautiful—who's to know they're also helping the work of this household to go ahead smoothly, joyfully, and simply.

STORAGE INSPIRATION

Here are a few bright ideas I've collected over the years for quick storage. Store rolled-up towels in a garage-sale wine rack, or a wire bike basket attached to the wall. Install a shelf about a foot from the ceiling; use it to store pitchers, punch bowls, and other large, attractive, but seldom-used items. Hang Peg-Board in your kitchen for utensils and pots. Hang all your baskets on one wall—use them to hold napkins and table linens. Refinish an old chest of drawers to hold videotapes, DVDs, and CDs. Use your creativity, and in no time you'll not only have some wonderful decorating ideas going— you'll also have some great storage spaces!

SPACE ABOUNDS

One of the first comments women make to me about home management is, "I don't have any space!" That's when you have to work smart! Here are some tips that work for me: Install a towel rack on the inside of the linen closet to hang tablecloths. Use storage boxes—stack them, and put a plywood round on top, then cover with a pretty cloth. Who will know? Use the tops of cabinets, hutches, and refrigerators to store floral arrangements or baskets. Build a window seat under deep-set windows and use the space for storage. Seldom-used luggage is great for out-of-season clothing. And by the way—you may have to toss some of that stuff!

PIECE of CAKE

Let's make shopping a piece of cake! By all means have a list ready—and stick to it! By getting in and out of the market quickly, you'll save yourself a lot of money. And definitely shop early in the morning—or late at night. Avoid the peak hours. Are you hungry? Then don't do any grocery shopping! You'll end up with a lot of stuff you didn't need—and probably shouldn't have! Buy your snack foods in bulk—it's cheaper. You can divide them up later with zip-lock bags. If you're buying clothes—take along a friend who's positive. If you're parking in a huge parking lot, tie a ribbon on your car antenna. If you're gift buying, how about a gift certificate to a portrait studio? Parents will love it!

QUIET TIME

When was the last time you had some quality alone time? It doesn't have to be a large block of time—15 minutes here and there can do wonders. Ask a neighbor to watch the kids for that window of time, sprinkle a few bath crystals in the tub, enjoy the solitude.

Stake out a table in a quiet coffee shop—or park your car under a tree. Enjoy a time of quiet with the Lord. Schedule longer quiet times too. Read your Bible, pray, write in your journal, read a book—refresh your mind and restore your soul! It sounds simple enough, but why don't we do it more often? We plan for so many other things, but we often forget this very important piece of time for ourselves.

REFLECTIONS

What does your home say about you? Oh, I'm sure it's neat and clean—most of the time. At least that's the goal. And if you're expecting guests, there may be fresh flowers, candles, special place settings for the table. Guest towels. Special soaps. But setting all that aside—what else does your home say about what you value, what you treasure? And not just for show either. I'm talking about the Bible on your nightstand. The verse you've got in a frame in your kitchen. The books on your bookshelf. Even the artwork. What *does* your home say about you?

TRANSFORMING YOUR SURROUNDINGS

As a woman, you can transform your surroundings! In this violent and impersonal world—women can make an impact for good. For gentleness. For grace. We've always had the ability to transform our surroundings. To make them comfortable, inviting. To bring comfort and joy to family and friends. I believe we should rejoice in those gifts and make the most of them! A beautiful godly woman is disciplined, discreet, gracious, controlled. She's got it together! "An excellent wife who can find? For her worth is far above jewels" (Proverbs 31:10). This is true for all women with integrity and godly character. Strength and dignity are your clothing. When you open your mouth in wisdom and you are a woman who fears the Lord, I say let's celebrate!

DESIGN SECRETS

Do you use a simple table and chairs for games, snacks, and puzzles? Give it new life by covering the chairs with a bright fabric. Or pick up one of those chrome kitchen tables from the '50s. Shelving and cabinets are an important addition to those activity rooms. Try using a miniature stepladder to hold family portraits. Placed on its side—almost anything can be a shelf. Baskets, crates, even bricks and boards. You can hide exercise equipment behind a screen or just let it be part of the room. Just remember—when you decorate these common rooms in your home, give them a creativity that nurtures the spirit as well as comforts the body!

SURPRISING VALUE

Who's the keeper of the simple treasures in your family? My friend tells of the time she helped a friend move to a new house. So much junk and stuff accumulated over the years. As the day progressed she was feeling so proud of what she'd accomplished for her friend. The truck was loaded and ready to head off to the new condo. Suddenly an anguished cry filled the air, "Oh, no! You didn't toss *that,* did you?" Her friend was completely distraught. *That* turned out to be the sorriest-looking trash can you could imagine—and a valued family treasure! It was a trash can decorated by their then-six-year-old and was a prized family possession. I understand perfectly. Our treasures are something to be cherished for a lifetime. Yes, even an old trash can! And what's wrong with *that?*

PLAN *to* SUCCEED

Time management is so important, especially if you want to live a balanced life. "Successful people do what unsuccessful people aren't willing to do." To get the most out of life, you have to make wise decisions based on what life means to you. Live life with a purpose—God's purpose. People don't plan to fail, but we'll fail every time if we don't plan to succeed. Success doesn't come by luck or accident—it comes because we schedule a plan and plan a schedule. Even getting organized requires a focus and a sense of what is important. We get that direction and truth for our lives when we stand firm in God's truth and hope for us.

GOD KNOWS

God knows the end from the beginning! My problem is, I hate to wait! I once heard it said that God gave women the last few weeks of pregnancy to make labor seem worth it. Ha. Waiting is one of the important lessons children must learn if they want to be mature adults. Instead of getting their way "right now!" they must learn to wait their turn so that order can be maintained. There's a time for snacks, a time to play, a time to nap. A time out. As adults we also have important times of rest, renewal, nourishment, and waiting. In your waiting periods, God often has specific work for you to do—work you might never accomplish otherwise. Trust the Lord. And remember He is in charge of all your days!

DECORATING

Here, wherever it is, is your spot.
This place should be expressing
something of yourself.
It should be communicating
something of you to your
visitors, but it should also
satisfy something within you.
You should feel "at home" here,
because you have made it
home with something of
yourself.

—Edith Schaeffer

ime is a precious gift in our lives. It goes by quickly. It can be spent wisely and sometimes unwisely. When we discover how to manage our time by managing our actions, decisions, priorities, choices, and opportunities, we are freed to live lives that are more abundant. Why spend time worrying about where to stack your latest magazines when you could be planning an activity with your kids or spending some quality quiet time.

When your surroundings are beautiful, inviting, and suited to your tastes, you are better able to focus on the elements of the heart—compassion, renewal, strength, and inner beauty. Proverbs 24:3-4 says it all: "By wisdom a house is built, and through understanding it is established; through knowledge its rooms are filled with rare and beautiful treasures" (NIV). It is easy to think that creating a welcoming home is all about the items we buy or how much we spend to arrange those items. But a true home has a foundation of heart and soul. A rich home is built by wisdom with spaces created through understanding what people need and enjoy. Let's create a home that overflows with rare and beautiful treasures of faith and love and kindness and hospitality.

Your **Personal Style**

UNIQUE *and* UNFADING BEAUTY

To be a woman of God doesn't mean you have to follow a cookie-cutter style. Women have always had the ability to make their surroundings comfortable and inviting. Rejoice in that ability. Make the most of it! Being a woman has little to do with how you dress or how you clean your house or how successful you are in your career. The Bible says beauty should not come from the outer you—but from your inner self. First Peter 3:4 calls it "the unfading beauty of a gentle and quiet spirit" (NIV). I love that! Don't sell yourself short. Reflect in your life—in your very presence—all that God intended you to be!

FAITH LIFT

If you're looking for a few simple tips to lift your spirits—these ideas can get you started. Make a few decorating changes, and you'll be surprised at how much it will lift your spirits. Hang or place a basket or two—or twenty for that matter!—from the kitchen ceiling, over the fridge, or on the floor under your kitchen table. Take some time to read a favorite passage of Scripture. Call a friend and talk about it. Pray together for a few minutes. Got some cookie dough in the freezer? Invite your neighborhood kids to drop by. Now that will lift your spirits like nothing else. What brings you pleasure? Share it with someone else today!

DECORATE *from* YOUR LIFE

Home decorating doesn't have to be a chore. Use what you already have. Before you hire an expensive decorator, take a look around. A collection of things your children have created makes a great display. Try matting a group of your son's or daughter's paintings and hang them in your office or your hallway at home. Buy a special bookcase to display those clay sculptures and Popsicle-stick creations. Arrange baby clothes and favorite toys in a shadowbox. Be creative. You'll be amazed at the praise you'll get for your clever decorating style. Make your home say something significant about you—and the people who live there. There's more to decorating than meets the eye!

KEEP ON GIVING

Today it's all about "leftovers." Not food, but bits and pieces of "stuff" that do double duty. Wallpaper pieces for gift wrap. Leftover paint to touch up a gift basket or thrift-store find. Don't waste anything. It's amazing what you can do with leftovers! The vintage jewelry you've been meaning to wear—but never do. It'll make a wonderful gift—even for a teenager! I have a friend who hasn't purchased a gift in years. And yet everyone loves to receive a piece of her wonderful jewelry. And she is so careful to wrap it lovingly and creatively. Anyone who receives her gift knows it has special meaning. Now that's a *leftover* you can give me any time! Just keep it creative—and "keep it simple."

RIGHT *in* FRONT *of* YOU

Don't spend your time thinking about what you *don't* have. Count your blessings for what you *do* have! And by all means—be creative! A friend of mine finds great delight and enjoyment in finding a good buy on vintage clothing. It's not only a hobby—it has given her an incredible wardrobe. Or taking old furniture and making it new. Or a family excursion in your own city. A friend of mine decided to get to know her city—to eat in the restaurants, visit the museum. She even took a bus tour. Don't sit around thinking about what you don't have. Plan to do something that costs very little—even if you *can* afford it! It's a great way to turn knowledge about your home, your community, your area, and your blessings into an understanding of your own style.

PRIVATE SANCTUARY

It doesn't matter how big or how beautiful your house is—someone else will have one that's larger and better. So what's a gal to do? Where do some people find the time for "house beautiful"? Or "house perfect"! Maybe your focus needs adjusting. I know mine does at times. Concentrate on what makes your home a loving, caring place for your family. No matter how little or how much you have, you can experience a godly home. Make it your sanctuary in the best sense of that word. A place where your family feels trust and comfort. And that comes from you. There's no house in the world—perfect or otherwise—that can replace you!

NEVER ORDINARY

My friend's mother used to say, "Do whatever you need to do—but always with flair." My kind of woman! Each day that God gives you is a gift. Make the most of it for yourself and for others. A meal doesn't have to be ho-hum. Put some flair into it! A little dash of the unexpected. When you're putting on your outfit for work, add a little sparkle with a special pin. You'll be surprised at the reaction you'll get. Pleasantly surprised! Put that same sparkle into your quiet time. Play some music in the background. Find a comfortable spot to enjoy a cup of tea or a favorite flavored coffee. In other words make the day special. It's a gift!

A SEASONED HOME

Transform your home into a seasonal masterpiece. In the winter, adorn your home with snow globes, pine cones sprayed white, sprigs from fir trees, and red ribbons tied to doorknobs throughout. Spring is a great time to awaken the senses with touches of color from fresh flowers, a fresh coat of paint, or fresh fruit in a bowl as a centerpiece. Bring the soothing warmth and gentle breezes of summer to your style with light and whimsical curtains, lemonade and iced tea in large glass pitchers, and a garage-find rocker painted yellow and set out on the front porch. In the fall, put a pumpkin on each step leading to your entryway. Fill a basket or large bowl with gourds, leaves, and pine cones for a beautiful fall centerpiece. May each season be a reminder of your gratitude for all that God has created!

LOVELY *and* LOVED

Most women have a wardrobe mostly made up of simple skirts, business suits, and jeans! But I still say—take time to be a lady! There's nothing better than gentle, feminine strength. Being a woman of God is a privilege—something you can give to yourself and to the people around you. We've always had the ability to make our homes and our workplaces inviting. So rejoice in how God has made you.

And as a woman of God, be a pacesetter. When you express your loveliness, you also reflect how you are loved by the Lord. Don't sell yourself short. Reflect in your presence what God intended you to be. Now that's feminism I can support—with all my heart!

RENEWED

Some of the best decorating ideas are those that transform the ordinary into the *extraordinary!* I have some ideas you can start using today; you can transform just about anything into a creative piece of art. Begin with the wonderful drawings your children make. Get them off the fridge and into frames. You'll be the envy of all your friends—to say nothing about the smiles on the faces of those little ones of yours! Leaves from your yard look great in an autumn frame. Use your imagination. Most importantly, apply the principle of transformation to your *life!* The Bible says, "Be transformed by the renewing of your mind" (Romans 12:2 NIV). That's something else you can begin doing today, and it will change your heart for a lifetime.

GIVE *of* YOURSELF

What is it about your house that makes it the "in place" to be? More often than not, it's the simple things that make all the difference. A guest book for visitors to sign, flowers at the doorway, a potted plant on the porch. And now you can buy so many wonderful flags for outside your home to celebrate the seasons—*and* your personality. When you have guests, put together little welcome bags with the guests' names on them. For a child, put in an apple, a pack of gum, crayons, and some paper—or a little picture book. For adults, place in the bag a travel toothbrush, a chocolate truffle, a crossword-puzzle book, and maybe a computer-generated certificate for a special, homemade breakfast. When you use your creativity to help celebrate the joy of another person, your house becomes a home to everyone.

A NEW LOOK

Have you ever considered how you can use personal style and perspective to change your decor? Here are a few examples to get the creative juices flowing. Use a glassed-in bookcase that holds knick-knacks—in your bathroom! Place a single chair by the bed to serve as a nightstand. Bring garden furniture inside to add style to one of your rooms. A stepladder can hold shelves or display family photos. Any old furniture can be painted, refinished, or covered. Don't be afraid to be a little outrageous; you can always change it if you don't like it. When we learn to see creatively, a whole new world opens up to our imagination. I love Psalm 66:5, which says, "Come and see the works of God, Who is awesome in His deeds." Through God's eyes, we can see life anew.

GLAD HATTER

I saw a front-door decoration that was made up of a hat and silk flowers. Those baseball caps are a great way to express your family personality. Hang them in your family room where everyone can see them. And how about hanging a beautiful retro hat inside an empty frame or on a decorative peg in a guest bedroom. The idea is to have fun decorating with what you already have. It's not only a way to liven up the place—it's a fun project for you and your daughter or granddaughter. I've found these fun together times to be a great way to find out more about the children in my life and how they express beauty. It's not about decorating—it's all about adorning your relationships with love and joy.

EXPRESS YOUR BEST

Your home is an expression of who you are. If that's a scary thought, just stay with me! It doesn't matter if it's a small apartment, a condo, a large home in the suburbs, or a room in someone else's home. It should reflect your special, personal taste. Fresh flowers don't cost very much, and they add a dash of color and sparkle to any room. Let your imagination be your guide. If you're on a tight budget—I have two words for you: spray paint! It works wonders—for old frames, old furniture, and walls. For a couple of weeks, spend one minute a day considering the feel and look you'd love to have, and then create a vision from there. We all need a place where we belong, a place where we can go to unwind and regroup. When we create this environment, we can begin to share our lives with others!

WHAT YOU LOVE

In so many cases, the most beautiful choice, home, or style is also the simplest one. Making beauty out of the ordinary brings joy—just in itself. An afghan that was once just a ball of yarn. A beat-up old table painted in a bright, happy color. Cost, size, and possessions have little to do with it! In fact, if we own too much, we can easily get to the point where we're merely a keeper of things. Surround yourself with what you love, and reveal your style with the smallest touches. When you aren't sure what to do next, trust your personal creativity. If you have never explored your style, this is a great time to begin. A little lace here, a basket or a candle there, and you've got the start of a new look—*and* a new outlook!

TOUCH *of* HOPE

Add a touch of hopefulness to your environment. For starters— take a cup of tea and wander through that room where you spend a lot of your time. Whether it is an office, a family room, or your kitchen, examine the colors and the arrangement of furniture. What is there about the room that makes you feel energized, ready to move forward? Pictures of your family? A memento from a special trip? Light coming through the window? Music in the background? Lit candles, or flowers sitting on your table? Simple as it sounds—all of these things can build a more hopeful atmosphere. When you are encouraged by the hope that comes with trusting God, your home will show it. Don't just save such a feeling for guests who come through your doors, but shower yourself and your family with the joy of a cozy, luminous home base.

COZY UP

It's *that* time of year! A time for a fireplace and everything cozy! There's something about wintry weather that appeals to me. Okay, so living in Southern California may have something to do with it! But even at that—I love a fireplace, with the chairs and couch arranged before it. Hot tea on a chilly morning or evening. Some flowers, a candle. It's not about the decorating. It's all about communicating. I want our home to be a gathering place, cozy in the sense of family and friends. Cherish those moments with the people you love. Over the years, it's what Bob and I and our family remember the most.

JUST THINK *of* IT!

Imagination makes all the difference. I love making the tops of dressers, tables—just about any surface—a piece of art. Decorators call them tablescapes. It's simply an arrangement of a group of items you love. A set of teacups in the guest room, a display of photos on the piano, a bowl of flowers. It's the little touches that will make your home special—a place you enjoy, a spot that says to your friends that you clearly live here and make your home here. Your life is a lot like the tablescape—how you are perceived, the way you conduct yourself, the words you say, and the life you lead are all displayed before the Lord and before others. Simply put, you can distinguish your life in Christ and reveal how He has given you a unique way of doing everything—from creating a home to embracing new possibilities.

YOUR LEGACIES

One woman's trash is another woman's treasure! Actually I said that to get your attention. It makes me shudder to think *any* of my treasures would remotely resemble trash. The kind of treasures I'm referring to are those things that bring to mind loving relationships. An old scarf that belonged to your grandmother. Your dad's Bible. Your mother's gloves or an aunt's favorite piece of jewelry. Old photos—or new photos for that matter! Don't bury them in dusty boxes. Bring them out where you can enjoy them. Share them with your children, your grandchildren. Look about you at anything you cherish that is a part of your history. Consider the joy it will bring your children some day. Those treasures are part of your special heritage and legacy. They tell *your* story.

REFLECTIONS

How are you reflecting your personality? I thoroughly enjoy infusing my personality into everything around me. It's not out of arrogance—at least I don't think so! It's because I want others to see Christ reflected in my life, in my surroundings. Pray over your house. The way you communicate with God is between you and Him. The wonder of this personal, intimate relationship is that it radiates from your very heart. My Bible is always out, not for decoration, but because I make reading His Word a part of my daily living, and I'm always willing to share that part of my daily life with anyone who enters our home. Make it a practice to reflect your faith openly and with grace to the people in your life.

Gracious Living

ISN'T IT ROMANTIC?

Excuse me while I check out your bedroom! For some decorating ideas, that is. The bedroom is where you spend a lot of time, so make it special. If you like a lot of fabric—go for the canopy look. If your husband isn't quite ready for that much fluff or it's too much for your tastes, you can create the feel of a romantic bed-and-breakfast by using a small, antique bookshelf or even an old trunk as a great nightstand. What you want to create is a quiet spot for prayer, to read, or just to rest for a few minutes. This is so important for your busy days. You don't need to have a whole room changed to feel the benefits of romantic living. Choose a chair in a fabric pattern that makes you think of a bouquet of your favorite flower. Light candles on the dinner table. Gracious living is felt whether it is created in small or big ways.

HATS OFF *to* GRACIOUSNESS

Have you ever watched movies from the '40s and '50s? Women wore such extraordinary hats. They were dashing and stylish. Bring hats back to life by making them a part of your home organization. Hang a straw garden hat to hold your tools and seed packets. Place an old bonnet with a little purse next to an antique photo. Make it fun and enjoy the results. The idea is to make your home a place that reflects comfort and graciousness. I have friends who live in the south, and they are so good at living with grace and hospitality. It is not just a lifestyle but becomes the very fabric of who they are. Whether you wear a hat or place it in your bathroom and fill it with luxurious shower gels and facial treatments, add that gracious flair to your life.

FRAMED *and* FABULOUS

It doesn't always take a lot of money to make a difference! You can have a charming atmosphere without spending a lot of money. Don't get me wrong—money helps. But sometimes there just isn't enough to go around. Remember, pillows, baskets, candles, and flowers are all wonderful items of interest and charm! And their cost is relatively low. Check out sale bins, and stop by a Saturday garage sale. Be sure to let your friends know what you need. One of them may have just the thing in *her* garage. Be creative. Use photos for framing, or adorn walls with elegant empty frames to showcase a still life. For example, objects from your kitchen-utensil drawer can look great on the wall. Just keep it inexpensive, and have it suit your personal version of gracious living.

NEW LIFE

Look around you. What do you see? I love to repurpose items in my house. A teacup becomes a lovely little flower container. An old hat transforms into a wall decoration. A bright red vase becomes the perfect accent piece on the mantel. My friend Adrian had a gorgeous red scarf. It was given to her by a special woman in her life. So she framed it with a sparkly necklace that belonged to her mother. Keep your eyes open. Take something you already have and give it new life. A new purpose. You'll feel revitalized—and your surroundings will take on a new dimension. It works for things of the heart as well! The Bible tells us to put on a *new* self—created in Christ Jesus!

IMITATE *and* IMPROVISE

When it comes to decorating your home, I have one word for you: imitate! By that I mean copy what others have already done successfully. Look over catalogs of your favorite home-decorating designs, check out showrooms that have just what you want—only can't afford. The other word for you is—improvise! I've said it before, "Style isn't what you *have*—it's what you do with what you have." That's true in just about every area of life, isn't it? Including the way God has decorated you in your own unique style. In that regard— there's no imitation. You're one of a kind. Make the most of what God has given you!

CREATE *and* CELEBRATE

I can't tell you the number of times a woman has said to me, "Emilie, I'm just not creative. I don't know where to begin when I am ready to decorate or organize." Actually you are undoubtedly more creative than you think you are! All creativity means is taking something simple and bringing it to life. Schedule some time for yourself to exercise a little creativity and stretch your imagination. What is it you'd love to try? Maybe it's scrapbooking—the kits help you get started. Maybe it's photography or writing or cooking. What-ever you're doing, ask yourself, "How can I give this an extra dash of creativity?" That includes not only things around your home but in your spiritual life as well! Soon you'll be amazed at how creative you've become, and you'll look for many other ways to express this newfound bit of your heart's potential.

SECRET SOLUTION

I received some great advice from an interior decorator that I will pass along to you: Put one thing that you just love in every room, and then build everything else around it. It could be something as simple as a favorite framed photo or colorful throw. Or more elaborate—like a piano or an heirloom grandfather clock. Whatever it is, it probably tells a story of who you are and what you love. We don't want to become overly absorbed in things—but there is something peaceful about being surrounded by reminders of what we love and appreciate. It gives us a simple setting for thanking God, for praying for those we love, and for remembering those who've loved us.

BRIGHTEN *with* BLOOMS

Infuse your life and your home with the blessings of creation. The best part about plants and flowers is that they create new looks in your living spaces with very little strain on your budget. Fresh flowers do the trick for me. I have them everywhere. If you have a garden—so much the better. In your kitchen, one little spray of flowers can brighten the whole area—and your day. You don't have to turn your home into a greenhouse, but a well-placed plant or flower will not only make you feel good, it's decorating with very little money spent. The point is, brighten your life and your surroundings. It's something you can do easily and inexpensively to make your day brighter. Be thankful for what you have, and enjoy what God has created for you.

LOVE *on* DISPLAY

Welcome home! Sounds great, doesn't it? With that simple greeting I've got some easy ideas for decorating your home. Right at the top of the list is: Use what you like! My friend says, "Sentiment is the soul of decorating." For her, everything has meaning because it was either left to her or given to her. Don't worry about a mismatch of styles. And don't be afraid to change things around. Bring out items you've had in storage, give your rooms a holiday or seasonal touch, or change out the pictures in your frames. There's something about keepsakes that helps pass along a legacy of family and home to your children and your grandchildren. Make your home a place where love is on display at all times. It makes such a difference.

SHOWCASE MEMORIES

Stick to the basics—especially when it's something you treasure. Matthew 6:21 says, "Where your treasure is, there your heart will be also" (NIV). And I've got a few ideas to share about those things you treasure! They tend to be symbols of our values, don't they? Love, joy, beauty, family. A delicate set of dishes, an afghan from your grandmother, a child's drawing, a watch; these are all treasures because they bring to mind loving relationships. These sweet memories can be a part of your home's essence and style. Go through your storage boxes, old photos, even your grandmother's Bible. Begin sharing these things with your children or grandchildren. Dust off the old scrapbook, bring out the quilt you love. They represent your heritage. They tell your story. Then pass them on to those *you* love!

CREATIVE DIMENSION

Creativity doesn't always have to be original. But my advice— always—is to keep your efforts simple and enjoyable. Gather great ideas from books or magazines—or borrow an idea from a friend. This isn't cheating—it's a smart step toward gracious living. Creativity is not only fun and pleasure filled, but it stimulates more creativity. The more ideas you collect—the more creative you'll be in adapting those ideas and coming up with your own different ones. Exercising creativity is one way to use the gifts and talents God has given us. It adds a wonderful dimension to life. And it makes us grateful for the ways we're different—the ways we're unique. We're made in God's image, after all! How much more creative can you get? God has made each of us a "work of art."

HOSPITALITY

The secret to decorating your home is to stick to the basics. Whatever you do to decorate your home, don't forget that the most wonderful adornment will be your spirit of hospitality—your willingness to share your home, your life, and your faith with others. And don't wait until everything is just right because as long as real people are in your house, that won't happen! Something will always need fixing, painting, or covering. Share your hospitality anyway. Invite friends to share what God has given you. We are to extend hospitality and love to those around us. The truth is, your home will always be its most beautiful when you stretch out your arms to express a gracious welcome.

REFRESHMENT

Proverbs 31:27 says, "She watches carefully all that goes on throughout her household and is never lazy" (TLB). If you're spending time in your kitchen—make sure you like what you see. Get rid of the clutter. I use "overflow boxes." Seasonal items such as Thanksgiving or Christmas dish sets go into the box for storage in the garage. If your kitchen's drab and boring—do something about it. Paint's the cheapest decorating tool there is! Fresh paint, a few flowers, some fun accessories, and your kitchen looks like new. Give it a look that is appealing to you and your family. Who knows, you might even get a few volunteers to help out with painting or other decorating measures. The idea is to make your surroundings fun and enjoyable. Refresh your home and refresh your spirit.

TOUCH *of* THE ORDINARY

Today take something ordinary and make it into something special. Nurture that creative part of you that is so God-given. And I'm not talking about arts and crafts. Sometimes it's as simple as putting extra effort into wrapping a gift for a friend. It says, "I care about what makes you smile." Other ordinary touches that offer extraordinary kindness are letters or notes "just because," a framed verse of Scripture for a friend, a recipe sent to someone you've just met, fun little surprise gifts in a lunch bag, or preparing a favorite meal for your family. Creative sharing is merely turning the ordinary into something special!

REUSE *and* RENEW YOUR LOOK

I have a friend who's great at recycling. She can think of more ways to use the same object than anyone I know. Before throwing away something that's broken or worn, consider how you might reuse it. A cracked mug makes the perfect vintage flowerpot. Worn-out jeans—have you seen the incredible rugs people make from old clothing? How about draping your worn sofa with a bright quilt? Or sharing some of your fun jewelry by giving it away as gifts. It's all in the presentation! Exercising creativity—yes, even recycling—is one way to be responsible stewards of the gifts and talents God has given us. Recycling is truly a way to bring a gracious warmth to your decor.

A ROOM *to* LOVE

Let's look at the kitchen for this quick moment. These days, meal preparation can be so simple and fast. So eliminate all that outdated stuff you don't like or use. Make a list of new things you'd like to have. Those kitchen "wishes" make great birthday and Christmas-stocking stuffers—for you! Make your kitchen a room you enjoy instead of one that is always about function and not pleasure. A fresh coat of paint, new cupboard handles, baskets hung on the walls, and even a few new pots and pans will give this frequently used room a great makeover. We spend so much of our time eating, preparing to eat, and cleaning up after eating—why not put a little effort into making that room a great place to be! This is a way to be gracious to yourself, and you will appreciate that effort every time you step into the kitchen.

TRUST YOUR STYLE

Want to know a secret? A long time ago I gave up trying to impress people with my decorating style, and it really freed me up to find my own sense of beauty. I've found it much better just to be myself. My most creative, expressive self, that is! It's simply taking your tastes, your personality, and your things and showing them at their best. What are the things you love? The activities you enjoy? What colors do you like? Are you the cozy type? What makes you smile? You may not even know how to describe your style. So what? It's the warmth of your heart reflected in your surroundings. That's what counts. Pretend you're an interior decorator. What would you tell—*you?*

A GUEST'S VIEW

There you are—in the middle of your living room—wondering what to do to make it look fabulous! Work with what you have.

Build from the basics. It helps to pretend you're a guest in the room you want to decorate. Look at the room with fresh eyes. What's working? What's pleasing? What draws your eye? Look for items that just don't fit. Most importantly, decide the focus for your room. In other words, what do you want people to see when they enter? The focal point is the anchor—the center of gravity. Find that and you're well on your way! Not a bad idea for every area of your life.

CALLING *on* COURTESY

Is that your cell phone I hear ringing? Our phones are terrific time-savers—and great for keeping us connected. I'm not always convinced we need to be *that* connected, but we'll talk about that another time. Don't let a phone rule your life by interrupting meals or conversations—and I won't even mention church services or concert performances. Turn off your phone when you don't want to be disturbed. Or at least put it on mute if you do. I don't want it disturbing *me!* It's graciousness, courtesy, and respect that are at stake! Don't get me wrong. Cell phones and any other technologies are great communicating pluses—unless they interfere with our human connections.

DAILY GRACE

I know you're busy—but don't neglect to give attention to those everyday details that refresh your life. Like keeping a vase of fresh flowers at your desk or in your living room. Take a little extra time to add a dash of makeup when you are heading out for the day or greeting your family. When you welcome your family members home, take a moment to ask about their days, and really listen. It will calm them and the atmosphere of your home. Get over the idea you're invisible when you're running errands or picking up the kids after soccer. Your presence matters, and you are valued! The way you interact is important. I'm not talking about "best behavior" for special occasions. I'm talking about the "basics" of grace in everyday life with your everyday people and with yourself.

Sweet Simplicity

SIMPLY LOVELY

If you're wondering where to hang your hat—you've come to the right place. Hats are back in style. So wear them and enjoy! But if you've got some just lying around, use them for creative decorating. Hang a straw hat in an empty frame for a beautiful addition to your kitchen. One friend of mine uses hats—upside-down—as baskets for plants. Or make a conversation piece with an antique hat, a beaded purse, and an antique photo. The idea is to be basic and creative at the same time. Adding a little personal touch here and there nurtures who you are. When you do, you have a space where all the people you love just love to be!

THE FABRIC *of* YOUR LIFE

If you're getting ready for a holiday, there's a lot you can do in your home to reflect the season simply by using two yards of fabric. Use whatever pattern or theme you like—because the beauty is, you can change it all later. How about a new lampshade, pillow covers, or napkins? Gather a bit of fabric around a wastebasket or flowerpot. Cover a photo frame. Line drawers or cabinets. You can even use fabric to wrap gifts! There are endless possibilities. And have you taken a look at all the beautiful offerings in fabric stores these days? It is as much fun looking at all the choices there as it is pondering your choices at a candy store. Put creativity and energy into your home. But above all else, make it a place where God is honored and your family is valued.

PERSONAL SHOPPER

When it's time to find a gift for someone in your life, get personal! My friend searched everywhere to find a book her sister had read over and over as a child. She finally found it. And although she didn't personally make the gift, it was a treasure to her sister. When making a gift or selecting one, use your imagination. You'll be amazed at the ideas that come to mind with a little inspiration. Browse stores or go online and survey the many different categories of gifts and items. Then think about how those could become very personal when given to the right person. An old family ring reset for your teenage daughter. Vintage clothing—which is so popular right now—and vintage hats, and purses, even gloves. The idea is to create your own unique gift of love for a friend!

TREASURES *on* HAND

It may be junk to you—but to me? Pure treasure! Look around you. There are treasures everywhere. The possibilities are endless. You may have things in cupboards and closets you haven't thought about for years. Old glassware. Evening bags. Jewelry. Hats. A beaded bag in a shadowbox is high style in decorating these days. Displaying jewelry—out in the open—is such fun. My friend puts sparkly bracelets in a beautiful dish on her coffee table. When friends are at her house, they pick one to take home with them. Teddy bears? Put them in a corner of a child's room and enjoy them. Look with new eyes. That junk is really a simple item-turned-treasure!

SIMPLY CREATIVE

I've met very few women who actually think they're creative. And yet they express themselves and their personalities with creativity in their homes all the time. Think of it this way—creativity is taking a simple thing and bringing it to life. With a few tips to get you started, I know you can do it! First of all, schedule some creative time for yourself. It won't happen unless you do. Then use your imagination. Like putting up a friendship display of little gifts and mementos from friends and family. Showcase things you love—salt and pepper shakers, or teacups like I do. It's a lot of fun. Just take a look around you. There's creativity just waiting to happen!

THE GREEN SIDE *of* LIFE

Bringing the outdoors inside is one of the simplest ways to create a new look and a refreshing change to your decor. If you have not had great luck with potted plants, you can do all your indoor "greening" with flowers. Anything that holds water can be used for a bouquet or flower arrangement—old drinking glasses, teapots, vintage bottles. A simple arrangement is always the best! Two long-stemmed flowers in a bud vase can be elegant. So can a single blossom floating in a bowl. Or lay your flowers right on the table for a stunning centerpiece. Tie them in bunches with ribbon or wind them around candles. Use your imagination. God has given us incredible beauty to enjoy in His handiwork. And each time you arrange a display or walk by a fragrant gathering of flowers, it will be a wonderful reminder to praise and worship the Creator who made it all possible!

SHOW YOUR HEART

When you walk into Robin's house, your eye goes immediately to a huge and beautiful armoire. She's learned a simple decorating trick that we can all use. When you have one large item, it guides your visitor's eye to that focal point. Maybe it's a piano, a fireplace, a wrap-around sofa. If the piano reflects your love of music, why not emphasize that aspect of your room! Frame an old piece of sheet music and hang it on the wall. But by all means don't let that oversized TV screen be the focus of attention—unless it's in a den or a family room. Someone has said, "The best decorating seems to come from the heart—created by people who know who they are and express it!"

GATHERING MEMORIES

If you're a collector, that's a good thing! Well actually, let me clarify that. Stashing and piling things in corners or nooks of your home is not a good thing. Collecting is far more than accumulating things. Carefully tended to collections help us organize our lives, to assign meaning to what I call miscellaneous experiences. My collections are important to me. They're chosen for a reason. I've assigned to them a meaning—a memory. And each one is meaningful to me. I've discovered that collecting invites conversation; it promotes storytelling. And it draws others in for meaningful times of sharing the things you value and care about—not just your possessions but those gifts of memories that God has given each of us.

FILLING SPACES

If you've stared blankly at your blank walls more than once, then you know how baffling it can be to fill large spaces or those odd-sized wall sections that often surround doors, windows, or arches.

Paintings, prints, and photographs work great as lovely fillers and focal points, and they can be inexpensive and still very attractive. Look for items that express a bit of who you are. I know a sports fan who decorated his office walls with sports magazine covers in acrylic box frames. One of my favorite walls is filled with photos of people I love. For an office or special workroom, consider placing framed calendar prints that remind you of places you've traveled or even of places you hope to visit. Have fun—make your home more interesting and inviting.

THE TRUTH *of* STYLE

There's nothing more fun—or more satisfying—than making your home an extension of your heart and soul. Whether you are renting, have bought a new house, or are taking your time decorating an older home, you can find simple and inexpensive ways to express the mood, spirit, and heart you wish to cultivate. Here's a tip you can use: Window-shop at the most expensive stores to get ideas, and then shop around for fabulous bargains on items and styles that match your favorite looks. A great way to see what's new is to visit model homes. Just don't get any big ideas while you're looking! I say, "Style isn't what you have—it's what you do with what you have." That's true in so many areas of our lives. Simply put, God has "decorated"—gifted—you in a unique way. He's looking to you to make the most of those wonderful gifts!

DESIGNER'S TOUCH

Designer sheets. Not for the bed—for the living room! The extra expense is more than worth it because you're going to decorate an entire room at a very low cost. Cover sofas or chairs, make designer pillow covers. Line an antique armoire with sheets and put in shelves, a crystal lamp, your dishes, and special memory pieces. Your table can have a runner in the same print with a centerpiece of flowers in the same colors. Get creative! For the price of four sheets, a little lace here and there—you've got yourself a newly decorated room. Here's a bonus tip for today: Keep it simple and do with what you have! Your God-given creativity can transform your home into something quite lovely.

ORDINARY SPLENDOR

Creating beauty out of the ordinary brings satisfaction and fulfillment. Watching a beautiful afghan come from a basket of yarn—or a beat-up old table do a Cinderella act after the magic wand of a paintbrush—is exciting. It's great fun to serve brunch on plates you found at a garage sale or to display dinner for your family on a tablecloth you bought on sale or to pour fresh juice into an eclectic mix of crystal glasses you've collected over the years from estate sales. You can feed your friends and family with style and feed their sense of joy too. Creativity doesn't have to be totally original. Picking up ideas from books or magazines just stimulates more creativity. When we exercise creativity, we're using the gifts and talents God has given us. And it's such fun to see what you can come up with!

KITCHEN AID

Whether we fancy ourselves as cooks or not, we all spend a lot of hours in the kitchen. We might as well make it a great place to be. First of all, streamline that kitchen of yours. Eliminate all the outdated stuff you don't like or use. Make a list of new items you'd like to have and post this as your birthday list. Simple changes like a fresh paint job, new knobs on the cabinets, or a rearrangement of your counter items can surprisingly give the space a face-lift.

Sometimes, when I need more prep space, I throw my bread board on the stovetop and use it to grate or chop. Hang photographs if you have the wall space. Here's a bonus idea: get a picture taken of your family making a meal together—or even better, *eating* one together! Frame this and place it in a prominent kitchen spot. This image will make even washing dishes more enjoyable.

CLUSTERING *with* CARE

If you have the space, fill a living room with separate little groupings. Cluster your wing chair over by a little table with a lamp. A gathering of child-sized chairs and toys near the fireplace. Your husband's oversized chair with its oversized hassock. Put the magazine rack next to it along with a nice floor lamp. Several little tables can hold groups of photos and other conversation pieces. All your living room really needs is a comfortable space for everyone to sit and then one or two places more. It works in a large home or a tiny apartment. What matters is not the size of the room but the warmth and the welcome it provides for you and your family. What really matters are the stories and the memories that will be created there.

EYE CATCHING

Homey touches come from either pieces that are built into your home's design or from those extra elements you showcase with easy effort. If you have a fireplace, it is a natural focal point just waiting to be spotted by your visitors. Dress the mantel with simple extras such as long, elegant candlesticks, small vases, or gatherings of collectibles. For other areas of your house or even the main room, use plants, a teddy-bear collection, a framed picture of yourself with your grandmother, photos, and vacation souvenirs to liven up the space and make it interesting. And slipcovers! You can make incredible changes in your decor so simply. In winter months, toss an afghan over your sofa, and when not using it, store it under a table for a wonderful touch of texture and color. And here's a bonus tip for you: Instead of using a lamp table, stack wooden trunks or packing boxes next to the sofa; they provide storage and surface area with style.

CHEER *for* THE DAY

Here are a few simple ideas to cheer you on—and up! If you want some creative time to yourself—schedule it! Plan an afternoon to write, paint, dream. Surprise your family some evening and eat dinner in the living room. Or when it warms up, set up a card table in the back yard for a special candlelit meal. A little extra touch here and there can make a lot of difference—even if it's only to you. A ribbon around the dinner napkins or a single flower in a vase on the entry table or a sachet in a bowl by the bathroom sink—all these things can breathe new life into a room. Here's a bonus tip: Take advantage of a free hour to write a love note to your husband or to your children.

A CERTAIN STYLE

What does style have to do with it? Believe me, when it comes to decorating, the main thing is to keep your efforts under control. A long time ago I gave up trying to impress people with my decorating style. It is better to be yourself—your creative, expressive, beautiful self! Take your tastes, your personality, and your possessions, and present them to others by displaying them. What are the things you love? The activities you enjoy? What brings you pleasure? What colors do you like? Why do we love certain houses—and why do they seem to love us? It's the warmth of our individual hearts that we reflect in our surroundings. You're going to do fine. You've pretty much got that style thing going.

PRACTICALITY CAN SHINE

Let's be practical! I have a few questions for you to ask yourself *before* you start decorating. How often are you willing—and able—to clean your house? If you hate dusting, what's the point of all the knickknacks sitting around? Is there anyone allergic to feathers, wool, or other fabrics? What about the needs of small children or pets? Do you have special lighting needs? And then there's the question of storage. Will you be doing a lot of entertaining? You'd be amazed at the number of people who forget to ask the crucial questions...and then end up with a beautiful home that no one can enjoy—except maybe the decorator! It wouldn't hurt to do a little inventory with a friend before you start decorating. It helps to keep things simple!

YOUR STORED TREASURES

Cluttered rooms. Limited funds. Bare walls. Yep. You're ready to decorate! Don't laugh—but wherever you're starting, that's the place to start. The key to affordable decorating is creative seeing. Learning to see new possibilities in your old stuff. It's a matter of "beautiful uses for ordinary stuff"—and easy transformations for stuff you like but don't know what to do with! Go through every nook and cranny of your house, your garage, that storage contraption in the back yard. Leave no stone unturned in your search for usable items. Look for interesting things that could be framed or simply displayed on a wall just as they are. New ways to use tassels, hooks, drawer pulls—you name it. Are you getting the idea? I knew you would!

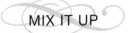

MIX IT UP

If you fall into the trap of comparing what you have in your home with that of someone else, you'll never be satisfied, and you'll never find your own simple style. Be encouraged to work with what you have on hand. Just keep to the basics and you'll have a great-looking home. For me, it's all about fabric. I can't resist a remnant table at the fabric store. My cabinets and storage boxes are bursting with a wonderful variety of material and trims. It's normal for me to have a mixture of patterns, hues, and textures. It goes along with my mismatched style. When I stopped worrying whether the overall effect was magazine worthy or like that of my neighbors, I realized the nest I had created for me and my family was just right. As long as the look is beautiful and tasteful to you, go for it. Express your personal uniqueness in your home. I guarantee that you're much more interesting than you think!

Design **Delights**

MAKE *a* STATEMENT

Here are a few simple ideas for decorating that big bare wall! First of all, think of your wall as a big, wonderful canvas. You're going to make it into an exquisite, decorative art piece. How about using it as a backdrop for a dramatic vignette—a glass shelf, an antique chair, a draped mirror. Or back furniture up against it—a sofa, chair, or armoire—lined with shelves or bookcases. The best part is, you can paint it—again and again! Instead of just rolling a coat of paint on a wall—try sponging it on. Paint the wall a bold color (if you dare!), or if you're artistic, do some freehand designs. The whole idea is to let your creativity out of the box. Remember, if you don't like it, you can always paint over it.

SWIPING INSPIRATION

My husband and I never had money for a decorator. But we always had our eyes open—constantly poring through magazines, looking for ideas that would work in our home. And I learned that "creative stealing" can be as valuable as "creative seeing" when it comes to decorating genius. Don't get me wrong—it's not shoplifting I'm suggesting! It's "stealing" ideas. Books, magazines, friends, anything to stimulate creativity. Without knowing it at the time, we learned valuable lessons in loving and decorating with what we had. And with each house, we learned a little more about who we are, what we love, what we value, and how we can share ourselves by sharing our home. And by the way—have you noticed? It's never finished!

TOP THIS!

Here are more ideas for using hats to decorate your home. Hang a hat as a "picture" inside an empty frame. It's a simple idea that will make everyone think you're sooo clever! Line up several hats over a window. In a child's room, hang a series of children's hats attached with clothespins to a line strung across a wall. Or stack a pile of hats in a corner or on a table. You can always combine a hat with silk flowers and put it on the door—inside or out! Or use an upside-down straw hat as a basket to hold a plant. If you have hats with a chin tie or brim ribbon, you can hang these upside down from hooks by the door to hold keys, gloves, a notepad and pencil—anything that tickles your fancy.

SPRINKLE WHIMSY

Where can you get the biggest return for the smallest decorating investment? In the bathroom! Not only are bathrooms great fun to decorate—you can add a lot of charm at the same time. Make your bathroom interesting and fun. Paint the walls, paper them, use a theme that you like and go at it! Don't hesitate to hang pictures in your bathroom—especially family photos. Mirrors and clocks are always great, along with ceramic pieces or silk flowers. Seashells in a bowl of potpourri. Lamps and candles are wonderful in a bathroom. Plants. Flowers. Tuck a little table near the tub to hold bubble bath and scented oils. The list is endless. No room is too small to surround yourself with things that turn daily routine into a celebration of pleasure.

FUNCTION *with* FUN

With a little imagination you can transform small objects into home decor! Shells, colored stones, old costume jewelry, Christmas ornaments, you name it. Try tucking them into open baskets, gathering them into matched jars, hanging them in boxes or bags. Use paint, trim, and creativity. You can transform an eyesore or utility item into a beautiful—or whimsical—part of your decor. Why not transform the dog's "dining" area into something humorous. Paint the end of one of your cabinets green, and add a little doghouse with the dog's name over the door. Place a little mat in front of it with the dog's food and water bowl. The idea is to have fun with what you see around you. And it doesn't have to take a lot of creativity!

THE PERFECT SPOT

Where do you place notes to your family? Where do you set the mail to go out the next day? What spot seems like the ideal surface to place the guest book when you have an open house? Don't have a perfect spot? Consider placing an antique bookcase in the entryway. Display framed family photos and other prized items on the shelves. Drape an elegant or colorful linen hand towel or table runner across the top. A favorite bowl—maybe one of your children's ceramic creations—or a teacup makes for a nice key holder. Keep a short stack of monogrammed stationery and a pen here also. Even if you don't have an official entryway, a slender bookcase will still be easy to fit somewhere near your front door, either in the hallway or in the living room. You'll love having a consistent place for communication, keys, and your favorite things.

YOU DESERVE IT

I'm guessing the most neglected room in your house is your work area or your home office. Am I right? Frankly, this room should be the cheeriest in your house. After all, it serves to inspire you. Paint the room in a bright color or, if you prefer, something soothing. Hide clutter in interesting boxes or baskets or behind drapes. And do something with those walls! Install an iron rack for hanging tools, or a pegboard for items you want to hang—anything from scissors to irons to art supplies. In other words, why not use the same creativity in your workroom as you do in every other area of your home? It's more than worth it if you're going to spend time there—make it a place you love to be! Create a space that feeds your spirit.

SPARKLE

Here's a simple idea for creating a festive table. Whether it's for the holidays or just to let your family know you care, be creative and have fun! Add a refreshing twist to your glass-topped dining table with just a little paint. Clean the underside with glass cleaner and use acrylic craft paints to dot colorful confetti directly on the glass. Or paint festive garlands around the edge—or a word of congratulations for a birthday or anniversary dinner. This same technique works great for any kind of glass—including the storm door or a coffee table or even glass plates. Just be sure to paint on the underside. A little bit of glass cleaner and you're back to normal. It's simple, but what a fun way to add a little surprise touch to your celebration.

FROM a CHILD'S HANDS

Be creative with your children's treasures. Incorporate your child's creations into your home's decor. It can be simple and amazing. Try matting a group of your daughter's paintings—hang them in your office or hallway. I remember hearing that Carol Burnett has saved every one of her children's drawings. They're framed and cover an entire wall of her house. Another clever idea if you don't mind being a bit bold: Provide a white wall in your child's bedroom, and invite them to use it for writing and drawing. Just make sure they understand it's limited to that one wall! Or buy a special bookcase to display clay sculptures and Popsicle-stick creations. Whatever you do, be creative. It's the simple things that are the most fun in your home!

LIVING COLOR

Dressed up or dressed down—color makes all the difference. My mother always said, "Once you've got the basics—just add color!" If the gold tones in your chair appeal to you, why not paint the ceiling in that same color? If you love the beautiful wood tones, let it serve as the palette for the colors you add to your room. And now find ways to add *living* color. Visit the sick, mow a neighbor's lawn, encourage a co-worker, volunteer at a local shelter, teach a Sunday-school class. When we lift someone else's load, we add color not only to our lives but to the lives of others as well. Surprise! I'll bet you didn't think *that's* where I was headed.

GOOD SCENTS

If you want to renew your home on a budget, the first thing you can do is paint your walls a different color. Change the room's complementary colors to match the seasons with new throw pillows, curtains, rugs, and accent pieces like vases and lamps. Have a decor element that runs throughout your house. For example, place seashells in every room, maybe on the window sills or atop furniture pieces. This is sounding easier all the time! A lot of people creatively use plants and flowers to enhance unused corners and higher shelves. And last but not least, fill each room with heavenly scented candles. It doesn't take much to make a change in the way your home looks and feels! It's really just a matter of keeping it simple and stylish.

PICTURE PERFECT

They're one of today's hottest decorating items, and they are everywhere. You probably have several unused ones tucked away in closets or your garage or attic. The wonderful thing about frames is that they come in all shapes and sizes and are made of various materials. There are glittery ones, glass, wood—anything you can imagine. But what do you put in all those lovely frames? So glad you asked! How about old postcards along with a picture of you and your family at Yosemite or some other favorite vacation spot. Children's artwork. Hats! Seashells you picked up at the beach last summer. Tiles. Even musical instruments. Just hang them on the wall, and then add the frame.

FLAIR WITHOUT REFINANCING

It doesn't have to cost a fortune—even a small one—to bring a little flair to your decorating scheme. For a creative touch in your bedroom, clean up a weathered old door from a flea market and add legs to it. With a few personal items arranged on the top of your new "table"—you've got that country look going! A fresh coat of paint does wonders for any room. Paint just one wall. It'll make a statement without overpowering the whole room. Your home—regardless of how much or how little you spend—is an expression of you. Make it one where you and your family come together to celebrate the most important things in life!

BORDERING *on* GENIUS

Do you have a collection of frames—with nothing to fill them? Think again! With a mat board you can create a wonderful organizer frame for your kitchen wall. In larger frames, place rows of wide decorative ribbon two to three inches apart on a mat board and secure each piece of ribbon along its base and sides to create little pockets for photos, ticket stubs, postcards, and such. Or paint your frames a single color and hang them as a group on a colored wall. It's like its own graphic—even if you decide not to put any pictures at all in the frames. And what child's room can do without a cork board for all their special "stuff." Just frame it! When you stick to the basics, it gives you time and energy for the really important things in your life.

THE RIGHT LEFTOVERS

What to do with all those leftovers? The leftovers I'm talking about today are *household* leftovers! Use wallpaper pieces for gift wrap and for covers for scrapbooks or boxes. Leftover paint is great for shelves, baskets, touch-ups. Cards are wonderful to use as artwork for your frames. If you're like me, you hate to waste anything! I even heard of a woman who took an old suitcase, cut off the top, and after it was lined, had the perfect dog bed. Even beads from an old necklace make great decorating touches for a lampshade or the edge of a picture frame. Check out your leftovers. Put them to good use. You'll be surprised at how simple it can be!

NEW LIFE

I love garage sales and flea markets. You just have to know what to look for—and how to use it. If you're fortunate enough to find an old milking stool, grab it. A little paint, and you have a new little table. Old-fashioned paper dolls? Arrange them in a frame for a young girl's room. The key to decorating with—do I dare say it—old junk is looking at items with a new eye. A marble-topped dresser can be a beautiful dining room cabinet. Gilded frames? Put them in the kitchen. With simple creativity, your home has new sparkle. And no one will ever know it's "junk"!

SECOND GLANCES, FRESH LOOKS

Sometimes the best idea for decorating is taking a second look! One woman said, "My collections on display inject a dash of color and originality into my home." How right she is. Sometimes an old treasure just needs a new container. Buttons in jars, a flowered hat under a glass cake dome, or old suitcases stacked in a corner make for wonderful new conversation pieces. You know the rule: If one thing looks good—multiples look even better. Jewelry on a pegboard, purses and hats on the wall of your bedroom. Let your imagination have a heyday. Give yourself time for those things that are most important in your life!

BRING OUT *the* FAVORITES

I love the TV programs where they take old treasures and turn them into something beautiful—and useful. It could be an old stamp collection, an old set of dishes—almost anything seems to spark ideas. No matter what it is you have, it can be revitalized and used in decorating your home. The best place to put these treasures is out in the open. Stack old books and Bibles on shelves and lamp tables where they can be read and enjoyed. Cluster a group of picture frames on a table. Spread quilts on your beds. Arrange framed art at varying heights on your walls to add more dimension to your physical spaces. Make your home a reflection of love and warmth—of giving and caring.

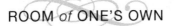

START DIGGING

When the sign that says "Garage Sale: Saturday morning" goes up—be one of the first to arrive. In this case, the early bird really does get the best "stuff." Some charity rummage sales have better things on the lawn than I have in my house! It's not only fun to look, but you can keep your eye open for that item you've always wanted. Keep a list with you of things that will complement your decorating ideas—or for gift giving later on. In the kind of throwaway society we live in, I find these treasure hunts simply refreshing and the perfect way to spend a rainy day. Okay—*any* day! Get out there and take a look.

ROOM *of* ONE'S OWN

We all need a place to call our own! And for me, that's the bedroom. Well, it isn't *always* my own—but you know what I mean. It can be more than a dressing room and a place to sleep; it can be a reading room, your own private retreat when you need one, and a place of comfort and connection. Make it comfortable and appealing. If you like the look of fabric—go with a canopy look, or an interesting headboard. And just about any small piece of furniture works as a nightstand. Or drape a cloth of soft shades of color over a round table. Keep the lighting soft and soothing. Make it a place where you can read your Bible, pray, write in a journal. Enjoy that special place.

Home Comforts

KITCHEN *and* LIFE EFFICIENCY

If you're spending more time in your kitchen and enjoying it less—it's time for a few simple changes. If space is part of the problem, store pots on a hanging rack. And definitely put like items together—spices, oils. Use baskets to help keep things organized. Spruce up your kitchen window with some simple glass shelves and plants. And you can brighten any kitchen by painting the ceiling white. Or install wonderful under-cabinet task lights. What a difference it makes! Or even a lamp for some soft lighting. Make your home a place where *you* feel comfortable. Store up your energy to use for the really important things in your life—your family!

STYLE *to* TALK ABOUT

The closer it gets to wintry weather—the cozier! I like it! One simple idea is to place your furniture so that people can talk without having to shout across the room. Furniture against four walls isn't warm or cozy, and the distance between pieces can make the room feel more awkward than guest-friendly. If you've got a fireplace, create a seating area in front of it—a sofa facing two armchairs and a coffee table in between. It's not decorating that's important—it's communication! Your home should be communication central for your entire family. Cherish those moments with the people you love. Over the years, these times are what we recall with the most joy.

STYLE SPECIFIC

It's all in the details! It's attention to those little details that can make your home sparkle. That old countertop sink in your bathroom—does it need an extra dash of style? Make yourself a skirted vanity by attaching a curtain rod to the frame. Then hang white cotton fabric or a beautiful print you can pick up as a remnant. In minutes you've brightened the entire room. This is proof that you can decorate with little effort. And thoughtful details will make your *life* sparkle, as well! Spend time in God's Word, listening to His still, small voice. As the Bible reminds us in 2 Timothy 3:17, God prepares us for every good work. Yes, it's all in the details!

GET COMFY

Is it old or new? And I'm not referring to myself! The look for fall decorating is old and comfortable. And it's the perfect time of year to bring out those afghans, the rich, warm-colored pillows you stashed away when the summer sun cast its light through your windows. One of the best inventions ever is distressed furniture. It's new—but it looks worn and comforting. Create a vanity-table corner in your bedroom, and add an old table and chair, a mirror, some candles, and a few flowers. Or use that old tapestry footstool as a place for a stack of books. Look around you! There are all kinds of ways to reuse what you already have.

GAZING *at* BEAUTY

I don't know about you, but I love to stare at beautiful things. And sometimes those finds are most unusual. One of my favorites was something I saw recently. Remember those old croquet balls we used to bat around the back yard? Well, imagine those colorful old croquet balls in a beautiful wooden bowl on your dining-room table! Or your grandmother's old clothespin bag filled with flowers on a kitchen wall. The idea is to keep an eye out for those discarded items that you can bring to life in your home and into your world. By giving an item a new use or a new place in your home, you will discover new ways of looking at beauty.

EASY TOUCH

If you want a friendly and inviting home, keep reading. Paint! Wallpaper! And some little extra touches will make your home sparkle! These don't have to cost an arm and a leg. Paint the walls in colors you love. Just the right color will do wonders for a room. Any room can be given a new touch of character with wallpaper either on all the walls, one wall, or as a border. Don't let your creativity stop at the walls. That sorry-looking old dresser becomes a decorator's dream with a coat of paint and some stenciling. And every bedroom needs a nesting spot—a place where you and your child or grandchild can curl up and read together. It's the little details in life that make all the difference.

A HOUSE *with* STORIES

Would you like to make your home more beautiful? Let your house "tell a story" of the people who live there. I love to mix my messages—so to speak—when it comes to decorating. I'll sprinkle a handful of glass beads on an antique side table—a reminder of that special vacation at the beach. I enjoy the glitter of an old glass vase against a mirror, a traditional flower arrangement on a modern glass table. Each item of beauty or feeling of sanctuary that you create will offer a story of hospitality, comfort, and godliness to your family and your visitors. But let's not forget that you can have a home overflowing with beautiful, expensive items and still not reflect the beauty found in the hearts and lives of people who love the Lord. In Psalm 149:4 we're reminded that "the LORD takes pleasure in His people." Share that pleasure with all who enter through your front door.

STENCIL IT IN

You see it everywhere—and if I can do it, so can you! I'm talking about stenciling. Have you attempted it? As kids, we did it by outlining block letters, using stencils. Now almost any surface is fair game for stenciling, including curtains. And by cleaning glass with water and vinegar before you begin—you can transform any glass surface. Don't worry too much! The fact that it's not perfect is part of the charm. And the more expert you become, the more delightful the results. It reminds me of the imagery in Proverbs 3:3, where it says, "Do not let kindness and truth leave you;…Write them on the tablet of your heart!"

WHAT POSSESSES US?

Collecting has become a nationwide mania! If you don't believe me, just check out *Antiques Roadshow.* It has become the most watched prime-time show on PBS. Or come to my house. Then there's everyone's favorite—eBay. They say their mission is to help "practically anyone trade practically anything on earth!" Baskets, quilts, old toys, new toys, furniture, folk art, tools, baseball cards.

Our garages and homes are overflowing. Isn't it interesting? *God's* emphasis for our lives is so uncomplicated. He says, "Sell your possessions and give to the poor" (Matthew 19:21); "God will supply all your needs" (Philippians 4:19); "[With] food and clothing...be content" (1 Timothy 6:8 NIV). Are we supposed to dump all of our possessions? Absolutely not. But we are called to keep the focus of our hearts on God, others, and our families and *not* on the next possession.

ADORNMENTS

"Button, button—who's got the button?" I'm using that old rhyme to direct your attention to some great decorating ideas using something as ordinary as a button. Here are some ideas for you to try. Use ribbons to go around a handmade card, get out the glue gun, and add a decorative button right in the middle. Or for a clever napkin ring, use fabric to cover a piece of cardboard, attach ribbon to go around the napkin as a tie, and decorate it with buttons—in colors to match your table. If you have buttons from your mother, grandmother, or even generations before them, find a way to keep the comfort of these heirlooms in your life. Add buttons to any scarf, table runner, pillow, sweater, or even a wide strand of ribbon to hang from a doorknob, and they will bring you great joy.

SMALL TOUCHES, BIG PICTURE

Let's explore how to make your home a little more extraordinary. This may seem simple, but just rotating pictures will give a whole new look to a room. Use seasonal frames if you can. A card table with matching chairs is one of the best investments you can make. Use it for patio or fireside dining, or for additional guests at a dinner party. Or use it as a semipermanent puzzle table. You'll be amazed at how fascinating a puzzle is to your guests. What matters is being able to sit and talk and play and share your life with your family and friends. Little touches can make a big difference.

DECORATING DEMOCRACY

Do you need a few tips on remodeling? Don't worry, we're definitely going to stick to the basics! (We just have a minute after all.) At the top of my list is making sure that anything you do complements how you live—how you entertain, including your needs for privacy or play areas. It's good to think through all of those issues before you begin any remodeling project. When you match your remodeling decisions to your lifestyle, you add comfort and function. If you never use the den for anything except a place to store boxes, get creative before you spend a cent. Think about the welcoming homes you have visited; how do they make use of their spaces? Ask your family how the room might be better used to serve their needs. Take a vote. Create a remodeling plan together and divide up tasks. It will be great to dive into decorating together.

SIMPLY *the* BEST

"The law of the LORD is perfect, restoring the soul; The testimony of the LORD is sure, making wise the simple" (Psalm 19:7). Isn't it interesting that I spotted a decorating article just recently with the title "Less Is Still More." The author said, "Simplicity is the highest form of sophistication." As soon as you get sidetracked by the "I wish I hads," your focus is turned away from what's really important. Mark 4:19 says: "The worries of the world, and the deceitfulness of riches, and the desires for other things enter in and choke the word, and it becomes unfruitful." Make the best and most of what you have. There is wisdom and perfection and restoration in God's simple best.

SCENTED PIECE

I'm always looking for household tips to make life a little easier. It works for me! Try spraying just a bit of perfume on the light bulbs. This will create a wonderful scent when the light is turned on. Or put one of those fabric-softener sheets in with towels or linens. Hmmm! Nice. I love using candles, and I find they last a lot longer if I put them in the freezer at least three hours before burning them. If you've got a bunch of dusty artificial flowers ready to toss, clean them by putting some salt in a paper bag and adding the flowers. As you shake the bag, the salt absorbs the dust and dirt. Works like a charm! If you want a new use for these flowers, intertwine them into a wreath, and place a floating candle in a pretty crystal bowl in the circle for a fabulous centerpiece.

COMFORT *over* COMPETITION

It doesn't matter what you have, someone else always has something bigger or better. And those decorating magazines can often give us great ideas but also a dose of the "gotta have it" syndrome. Maybe it's time to take a little break. Instead of focusing on "home beautiful," concentrate on what makes your home warm and caring. A place where you can express your God-given talents. No matter how little or how much you have, you can experience the results of a godly home. Make it more of a sanctuary in the best sense. A place of security, trust, and comfort. That comes from you. There's no decorating scheme in the world that can replace the role you play in your home!

STREAMLINED SPACE

I'm thinking simple and small—small living rooms, that is! If you want to create an illusion of space, start by getting rid of those table lamps. Use wall sconces instead. It immediately eliminates several pieces of furniture in a small room. And why have a three- or four-seat couch. Do any more than two ever sit on it anyway? Keep your windows simple and unfussy. The walls should be painted in light colors to give the effect of more space. And those items you love to have sitting around? Group them together. It's more interesting, anyway. The word "living room" says it all. It's the "room" where we live! Make it a place where you and your family gather comfortably.

GRACE ABOUNDS

Here are some decorating tips with a little something extra tossed in for good measure! When you set out to decorate your home, keep this in mind: Give yourself some time. Know what you don't want. Don't be afraid of color. Look for ways to save money. Show off your collections, and create a homey atmosphere with flowers, candles, baskets. The most important tip today may be this one found in 2 Corinthians 9:8: "God is able to make all grace abound to you, so that always having all sufficiency in everything, you may have an abundance for every good deed." Fill your home with a heart of goodness so that God's grace will abound. Kinda keeps everything else in perspective, doesn't it?

TROUBLE FREE

There's something missing—I just don't know what it is! Decorating is all in the eye of the beholder. But here are some things to try that might help when a room just doesn't look quite right. Try changing the lampshades. Remove the books you've got stacked next to that chair. Or change the curtains. That can spruce up just about any room. Remove some of the pillows—or change them altogether.

Even photographs should be rotated once in awhile. Change light bulbs. Maybe they need to be softer. Problem solvers—we all need them for the mundane stuff around the house and certainly in our lives. For me, a cup of tea, my prayer journal, and my Bible do the trick—every time.

EXTRAORDINARY

I saw a great headline the other day. It read: "Never Have an Ordinary Day!" Now that's my kind of thinking. God gives you each new day as a gift. Take a little time to make ordinary things extraordinary. A note to a friend doesn't have to be ho-hum. Add a pressed flower for her to enjoy. Or try getting up a little earlier. Spend those moments getting ready for the day in a quiet time with the Lord. Make lunch or dinner a "special occasion" at least once a week. You'll be surprised at the reaction you'll get. Okay, so you won't be surprised! Today is a gift; take pleasure in unwrapping it!

TAKE YOUR MEDICINE

Fresh flowers are such an inexpensive way of saying "Welcome." You don't need a dozen roses from the florist. If you want to make your home a welcome place for everyone who stops by, a bunch of daisies from the supermarket, an iris from your yard, or even a handful of dandelions from the curb can proclaim: "Love lives here!" Or hang a bright banner by your door to say hello, or—if you're really bold—paint that door red! It's such a privilege to bring a sense of joy and comfort to an otherwise rushed world of busy schedules and crazy lives. Remember Scripture says in Proverbs 17:22, "A joyful heart is good medicine." Be joyful today with a good dose of pretty flowers!

Beauty **Blossoms**

TAKE TIME

The next time you take a walk, pick a few flowers. Tuck them into a vase by your bed—on your husband's side. How about collecting those perfume-sample inserts from magazines—use them to freshen your drawers or suitcases. Make your closets reflect more of your personality. String one-inch white eyelet along the edge of your closet shelf. Attach it with a glue gun or a heavy-duty stapler. It's a great feminine look. If you wear a suit to the office—try the old-fashioned custom of putting a rosebud or a tiny bunch of violets on your lapel. Don't be so predictable—try it. It will reveal a whole new side of your personality.

JOY *in* VIEW

Did you ever grow a sweet-potato garden as a child? It's never too late. For that sweet-potato garden, get a quart-sized jar, and stick the potato in water and wait. Better yet, share the fun of growing a potato with your favorite child. And about that refrigerator! Make the inside a feast for the eye. Use see-through containers for fruit. Even a small bowl of flowers can bless the eye of anyone looking for a snack. It says "I love you" in a special, unexpected way. Or freeze grapes and roll them in granulated sugar. Store in a glass bowl or on a pretty plate and toss in a salad or use them as garnish. Yummm. The point is, bring joy to your surroundings.

SECOND CHANCES

Have you ever thought about treasure hunting in your own home? The key to affordable decorating is looking at that old stuff and seeing new possibilities. Start by going on a treasure hunt in your own home. Put a blanket in the middle of the floor, and empty out those storage cupboards. Pick up one thing at a time. Ask yourself, "Am I drawn to this item?" "Is it beautiful or interesting?" "Is there some way I can use it creatively to decorate my home?" Once you've gotten used to thinking, *Do I like it? Can I use it?*—extend your treasure hunt to other rooms. You might be surprised what close-to-home treasures you may find.

VINTAGE BEAUTY

All it takes is a bit of ingenuity to discover some wonderful decorating possibilities in your familiar old stuff! Any old furniture can be painted, refinished, or covered. Those old rusty TV trays—remember those? Paint them—you've got yourself some vintage eating tables. A child's wagon can become a planter. Drawers from a broken desk can serve as trays. Small drawers can hold plants or spice jars. A crystal salt shaker can hold a miniature bouquet on a nightstand. A collection of flowerpots can hold candles or potpourri. Learn to love what you have! That attitude will spill over into every area of your life. In Philippians 4:11, the apostle Paul reminds us: "Not that I speak from want, for I have learned to be content in whatever circumstances I am."

MAKE ROOM *for* SURPRISES

The decorating police won't arrest you for your lack of decorating skills! But if you are still too intimidated to start, maybe I can help. Always think hospitable, comfortable, and cozy. After that can come fashionable, sleek, and dramatic. But your dwelling, beautifully decorated or plain, must first function as a home. Strive for a home that is truly welcoming to the people who live there. Buy what you love—but avoid paying retail. Put something that is alive in every room—real flowers, green plants, a cocker spaniel! Try to stage a surprise in a room to delight the senses. It might be an oversized picture, a red pillow in a green room, a teacup on its side, whatever seems like a spark of the unexpected will brighten the mood of everyone who comes into this room. And don't put out everything you own. There's a fine line between cozy and cluttered. That's true in our lives too. When life gets too cluttered, we neglect the important things.

BEAUTY *in* TRUTH

"Don't use white—it shows dirt!" I have a few more decorating myths you can ignore. How about the myth that says, "It all has to match." A mix of styles, colors, and periods is definitely beautiful. It can be visually exciting. Just try to have a common element to tie them all together. "You need a sofa, a chair, and a coffee table." Who says you do? Think instead of what you need to happen in that room. Or how about, "The sofa goes up against the wall." Not always. Try setting some pieces at an angle or creating conversational groups away from the walls. Or how about, "Anything goes." Just a reminder—certain classical principles still prevail, in decorating and in life. Psalm 119:160 says: "The sum of Your word is truth." No myth there!

WHAT YOUR HOME SAYS

Where do I start? It helps to pretend you're a guest in the room you want to decorate. I know—a scary thought, isn't it? Look at the room with fresh eyes. What's pleasing? What draws your eye? Also consider a room's language—lighting, comfort, balance, and utility. Use color to tie a room together. Fill in with imaginative accessories. This is where you can have a lot of fun and also save the most money. With a little creativity, you can add inexpensive sparkle to your walls, tables, and floors. Also, decorating is more fun if you involve someone else. Don't forget to talk to your husband, your children, and anyone else who lives in the house. Their opinions count too.

A DASH *of* WONDER

Think of ways to make your life child-friendly—as well as child-proof! Tuck a basket of children's books and toys in a corner, and toss a few throw pillows beside it to make a welcoming place to play. Add elements that cast a bit of wonder over the room either with items, lighting, or your arrangements. In the evening, light a candle by the kitchen sink. The soft light can add a spirit of loveliness. Design a "love shelf" in your home to display those little creative gifts from friends and family that mean so much but don't seem to fit anywhere. Tie a ribbon around your table napkins—add a fresh flower, a few dried flowers, or a piece of ivy. A little creativity will add joy and beauty to the lives of you and your loved ones!

GARDEN GLORIES

Take advantage of all the wonderful flowers and herbs to put a little spark in your life. You know those bittersweet pots you find in a garden shop? If they don't match your pale pink or bright red window—buy white plastic pots and a can of spray paint. In minutes, you've got pots to fit your decor. In your kitchen window, a row of herb plants in three-inch pots will not only be decorative—it will also add distinctive flavor to those gourmet dishes you plan to serve. For your porch, fill an attractive pot with blooming fibrous begonias. Order ladybugs from a gardening catalog—let your children release them in your yard. Ladybugs are God's way of keeping harmful bugs under control—and kids love to help them "fly away home"!

SHADES *of* SERENITY

Color in your home can make a world of difference! Color can be used so effectively—especially if you need to redefine some of that space in your home. If a space is too large, add a throw rug in a complementary color, creating a "get together" spot. Add some soft-colored curtains for a change of seasons. The idea is to create some intimacy, a place that's inviting on a chilly evening or a spring afternoon. Decorators will tell you—the richer the colors, the more welcoming the space. Red! Go for it. And shades of cranberry, plum. Experiment out of your usual comfort zone. Your home can be a place that gives you a sense of quiet for thinking about the things that really count in life!

A CUSHY JOB

I love to have pillows everywhere. It warms up a room so easily and without a lot of expense. I've discovered oversized pillows are a lot more comfortable than the smaller ones. The more cushion the better. Here is a fun project for you today—take a survey of what pillows you do have and what styles might spruce up your rooms. Make sure your pillows are filled with down or whatever filler you prefer. You can even have your old ones restuffed! And don't be afraid to mix the patterns. Florals, stripes, bold colors—just keep them in your color scheme and go for it! In every room! You'll be amazed at the transformation you'll see in your living spaces. Make your home the kind of place you and your family want to spend time in!

COLOR CONNECTIONS

I don't know about you, but I'm always looking for easy ways to decorate and spruce up my surroundings. For example, add accessories to your tabletops that highlight color tones you've used in your room. You will be surprised how making just a few changes in your room can change your entire perspective and the complete feel of a space. Many are unsure what to do with their various collections. I suggest that you always arrange them in odd-numbered groupings. Three is the magic number! Cluster those things that have differing shapes. But keep the color theme going. For couches, keep the color neutral and add colorful pillows or throws. Layer all kinds of textures and fabrics. The link is the color. Isn't this fun?

EASY *and* EXCEPTIONAL

Use your cherished collectibles in unconventional ways. That old doorstop you inherited from Grandma? Put it on a side table. If you want a nice, rosy glow in your room—use pink light bulbs. Fill some spaces with old books. Or buy pictures based on a theme you like and go with it. Reflections from old mirrors or glass give a room warmth and interest. One of my friends antiqued a new mirror and put it in an old frame. Or use the mirror as a tray for your candles.

Look around you! There are wonderful things you can do—simply and without costing a lot. You'll love the results.

GREAT PARTNERS

Here are a few simple suggestions for "aging your home"! When everything's new and you want a bit more lived-in feeling, you can age the room. What does that mean exactly? One example of adding richness and history to an area is to use vintage pieces even if you have mostly new furniture otherwise. Who says that new and old can't create a lovely partnership. By adding a sense of a different era, you'll make your home look less "manufactured." Oil paintings, leather books, the family Bible, your favorite collections—all add to that "we've lived here for a while" feeling you want! The bottom line isn't just about having a beautiful home—it's about creating a place where you and your family can spend time with one another, a place where you are nurtured, a place where you can partner the good ol' days with today's adventure.

BATHROOM BEAUTY?

Don't hesitate to hang pictures in your bathroom. Plaques, posters, framed magazine covers—whatever strikes your fancy. Mirrors and clocks are naturals for bathrooms. Flowers are always a plus. Seashells are also at home in the bathroom. Put them in a bowl, hang them, or glue them to a frame. And my favorite bathroom accessories are lamps and candles! Scented candles and potpourri give everything a special ambience. Just don't stick to the typical. A few unexpected touches can make your bathroom unique. The accessories you choose for your home will turn daily routine into a celebration of pleasure. These simple little touches will help set the mood so you can think about the more important things God brings to mind.

LITTLE TREASURES

Hey, if little things can drag you down, then little things can also pick you up! For those little pick-me-ups, here are a few ideas. Always keep something green in a little vase or pot over your kitchen sink. And I'm not talking about cash—I'm talking plants! Find a small gift book that lifts your spirits, and take a moment to read it. Schedule a lunch break with an encouraging friend or an occasional time volunteering at a hospital nursery. Write favorite Scripture promises on sticky notes and post them on your bathroom mirror. Find a lovely place where you can walk to boost your spirits—a park, by the beach if you're fortunate, even a landscaped mall will do. Little things—simple things actually—mean a lot!

DECK *the* WALLS

Any room where you work is a room that needs a dose of joy and motivation! Sadly, these tend to be the rooms that are used more for storage than pleasure or that have bland walls and no decor and possibly no basics like curtains. Why not a red computer desk? You need function, of course. But you also need a little beauty. So don't neglect that workroom of yours. Paint it a bright color or something soothing. Hide the clutter in boxes or baskets or behind drapes. And deck the walls! Your office could have a wall of work-related cartoons or inspiring quotes. Give everything a face-lift. You'll be surprised at what a difference a beautiful workspace can make in your creativity and production. One other thing! I wouldn't do any of this in someone *else's* workspace without checking first.

FAMILY PHOTOS

Have you ever thought of your family photos as a collection? One of my tables has the photos of the women in our family. They cover several generations, and I display them in a variety of frames. The mother-daughter-granddaughter theme pulled the collection together. And no one can resist stopping and taking a peek. You can group all black-and-white photos or formal and informal in groups. Another idea is to keep the same frames but change the photos for the seasons. If you have a ton of photos—rotate them and enjoy your entire collection. And for a designer touch—add a surprise to your grouping—something that doesn't "match." Like an artichoke in a basket of apples! The idea is to share yourself with others in ways that are interesting and fresh.

$\mathcal{D}ecor$ with More

LET IT SHINE

Put two lamps of different sizes on a side table with books, a small clock, a pot of flowers, or a fun ceramic piece. It improves the look—and provides better lighting! Your coffee table is an ideal spot for a plant, even a terra-cotta pot for candles. For a softer look, add a throw rug made of mohair or wool—something warm and inviting. And I don't know about you, but I like bookshelves in the living room—complete with family pictures and a mixture of the things I collect. I also love to frame favorite scriptures to welcome me as I go from room to room. And what a great reminder of Christ in our lives when we have guests!

THE HEART'S GALLERY

"Just say cheese!" If you're like most women I know, you have at least one photo wall or shelf somewhere in your home. My entire home is practically a gallery. Walls, tabletops, refrigerator door—all crowded with the faces of people I love. My husband, my children, grandchildren, new friends, old friends—you name 'em and I'll display 'em! How precious they are to us, these gatherings of faces. And it's so fitting, isn't it? Because our family and friends' pictures tell the story of our lives. Cherish those friends, those moments. Hold them close. Seek them out, enjoy their company. Treasure their faces. But just as every friendship is unique—make room for new people in your life. Then place them in the gallery of your heart.

HOPE ALL AROUND

A little extra attention to your preferences can make a big difference in how you modify your surroundings. What colors lift your spirits? What kind of music makes you feel energetic or peaceful? Do any particular fragrances give you a sense of contentment—or remind you of fun times? Are any visual symbols meaningful to you? A flower? The face of a child? Do any scriptures or quotations stick out in your mind? Do you own any objects that make you smile? Maybe a gift from a friend, a special book, a silly memento. Are you getting the idea here? Surrounding yourself with color, music, and fragrances that appeal to you will help replenish you when your cup drains a little low. When hope is all around you, it's hard to be down!

SIMPLE WONDERS

Do you need some ideas to brighten your home? Tassels, ribbons, buttons, and old jewelry can decorate almost anything. Baskets can be painted, threaded with yarn, or used as is. A rusty mailbox can be scraped and painted or decoupaged. A child's wagon can become a planter. Small drawers can hold plants or spice jars. Old clothes? Make them into pillows, place mats, or other creative pieces. Almost anything can become a lamp—including a cracked pitcher or teapot. A crystal salt shaker can hold a miniature bouquet on a nightstand. I loved a friend's painted stepladder she used to display family photos. All it takes is a little bit of ingenuity and an eye for the unusual for some wonderful treasures!

A CERTAIN SOMETHING

What's your decorating style? Before you answer—remember, style is not what you have—it's what you do with what you have! Decorating with style is merely taking your tastes, your personality, and your possessions and showing their best face to the world! What you love, what activities you enjoy, how you work—these are all issues of style. My advice? Take a little journey of self-discovery. Shop in all the places you can't afford. I said shop, not buy! Notice the wood finishes, the fabrics, the color schemes. Look through magazines and clip out what you like. In fact, pour yourself a cup of tea, take your magazines, and start enjoying the journey through limitless ideas. It won't be long before you'll begin to see a picture of what your style really is. And that's the best place to start!

FLEA FACTOR

Garage sales, swap meets, flea markets, and estate sales are great sources for decorating magic! Just watch out for large-scale antique dealerships with inflated prices—and often poor merchandise. But these stores can be great sources of unique accessories if you know what you like. Just stick to your budget! I know of a church in our area where the rummage sale each year is one of the hottest spots in town for that particular weekend. You wouldn't believe some of the incredible bargains and wonderful pieces that are available. Keep an eye out for estate sales, auctions. A few weekends of treasure hunting, a little creativity on your part, and you may locate just the piece you've needed for your beautiful home.

SPECIAL FABRIC TREATMENTS

You don't need to be a professional seamstress to make beautiful use of fabric in your home. Forget the sewing—grab the glue gun! Fabrics are great to add charm and texture to your room. And slip-covers are like a magic wand. A simple straight chair covered with tulle, tied with a satin ribbon, is a wonderful touch for a bedroom. Or transform that folding chair by slipping a pillowcase over the back and tying the base with ribbon. You're laughing—but you try it! Fabric is a great revitalizer in your home! Speaking of revitalizers, when was the last time you grabbed a cold glass of tea, picked out a comfortable spot—Bible and notebook in hand—and spent some time revitalizing your heart? Go ahead—treat yourself!

LIGHTEN UP

Illuminate your world with candles, lamps, and other bright ideas! Lighting is one of the most important ingredients in making any home beautiful—and comfortable. There are all kinds of economical options. But let your imagination take over—with special lamps, mood-setting lighting with twinkles, firelight, warm-colored bulbs. Or miniature lamps, groupings of candles, wall-mounted sconces. I even have candles in my kitchen. Look around you for shining examples for lamps and shades. Like an old watering can, a cookie jar, a teapot (you knew I'd get that teapot in here somehow!)—or even old sports equipment. Light! It's wonderful. It so reminds me of the light we can be in the world—to our friends and our neighbors.

ART COLLECTORS

You name it, my friend Penny collects it! Oh, we're not talking junk or stacks of old papers sitting around. No. These are bona fide collections—some whimsical, others incredibly artful, all precious to her. That's what collecting is all about! One teacup is simply—a teacup. Two is service for two. But if you take those two teacups, arrange them on a glass shelf with a lace scarf, and perhaps add a third to keep them company, you have something that can brighten your living space—and spark your memories! I know a man who collects wooden yardsticks—they're hung all around his workshop. Whether traditional or offbeat—your collection tells an eloquent story of who you are and what you love. Now what's wrong with that?

NEW LEVELS

With a few simple tricks you can make your home more beautiful—even with a zero budget. Tradition says that wall decorations should be hung at about eye level. I'm here to set you free! Try hanging a picture higher or lower than expected. High over a bookcase, for example. Or try wall-hung decorations combined with a plant. Or a Raggedy Ann doll in a child's rocking chair can enjoy her own eye-level miniature painting. Or take the piece of art and set it on a shelf or table and just let it lean against the wall. The bottom line is to be creative. Break out of the box, and you'll be amazed at what you discover. That's true with life as well as with decorating!

SHAPING a LOVELY LIFE

All my life it has been my desire to live a simple life. I spent the first half of my grown-up life as a homemaker and mother, the second half running a business with my husband. Yet, the home we decorated together has been featured in *Better Homes and Gardens*. Who, us? How did we get to that point? I began as most do—with nothing and going from there! I have to add that the beauty and interest of our decorating is as much to my husband's credit as to mine. The whole idea has been to make it a beautiful place of love and comfort—a place to entertain new and old friends. And definitely a place that says God is part of who we are and how we live!

THE HUNT

I can't think of a better way of spending a weekend than looking for treasure! I love finding forgotten or hidden treasure. It's kind of like going through Granny's attic, where behind any box or stack of dusty items there could be an amazing gem. Garage and yard sales are great sources. Okay, so I'm hooked! Thrift shops can be great. If you're a regular, often the sales volunteer will call you when a special item comes in. Antique and home shows are also good for a rare find or two. Even if you can't afford what you see, it's a great education and lots of fun. My favorite hunting ground is still an old attic. Whenever I buy or use an object that's been used before, I feel I'm carrying on someone's heritage. It's what keeps me in Granny's attic even now.

A FITTING PROJECT

This is your day if you're looking for wonderful bits and pieces to use in decorating your home. Torn or worn linens or lace are great when recycled into pictures, pillows, and napkins. Pick up single lids and stoppers or even old teapots without lids. You may discover that two orphans fit together. Lidless items can always serve as vases and planters. Old, gold-leaf picture frames are a prize. Odd kitchen chairs can be refinished. Use them as a unique set. Miscellaneous plates and saucers can be combined on a table—with a stunning effect. Recycle old costume jewelry. Be quick to pounce on cabinets, trunks, and cases that can be put to different uses. It's the perfect way to spend a rainy day. Or for that matter—any day!

COME ON IN

Where in your house does everyone love to gather? I'll bet it's the living room or family room. Regardless of the size of your home—apartment or condo, motor home, or even a boat if you live in Southern California where we do—the "sitting room" is where family and friends gather. And it's the heart of your home. It deserves your most creative efforts to make it both beautiful and cozy. Besides, it's also where everyone will see and appreciate what you've done to make it comfortable. Whatever decorating scheme you use—remember you should always work toward nurturing the spirit as well as comforting the body! When you do that, you'll have a space where all the people you love, just love to be!

WHISTLE WHILE YOU WORK

Let's go back to your work space. Do you get the idea that I want you to have a splendid place to toil away? I think it is so important. Even objects like file cabinets, refrigerators, and cabinetry can be decorated to add cheer to your day. You don't have to be stuck with the look you started with. It is possible to have appliances professionally painted, and with great success. Kitchen cabinets can also get a face-lift with a coat of paint. Or remove the cabinet doors entirely and replace them with glass-paneled doors. Now that's a new look! Paint and paper the cabinet interior—line the shelf edges with lace. Or just try replacing the handles—what a difference even *that* will make! See, much cheerier.

PLAY *with* IT

A child's bedroom is a playground for any decor diva. There are so many options. Circus themes are a fun way to go. You can paint the walls and ceiling to resemble the inside of a circus tent. Use clown stripes for curtains. Or pick a nautical theme with ocean blue carpet and anchors and life preservers for decoration. Paint a tree trunk in a corner of the room for a wonderful fantasy of living in a tree house. You could even hang a little wooden swing from the ceiling for a doll or stuffed animal. We always kept plenty of storybooks to read and look at. There's nothing like sitting in your child's room, reading them fascinating stories out of the Bible. What great teaching times to have with your children!

THE SHAPING *of* CHILDHOOD

I love decorating children's rooms. You can let your imagination go to so many wonderful places. Try to provide a living space that encourages children to draw, paint, build, act, read, and create. An easel with a bucket filled with crayons or chalk is very delightful. A lap desk or a small table and chairs invites kids to sit and explore their creativity. Paint the back of the door with blackboard paint—or one wall with high-gloss enamel so children can draw on the walls. Or stretch out rolls of white paper for mural making. Bean-bag chairs, comfortable cushions, and a basket of books and toys will encourage reading. Decorating your child's room is truly a wonderful opportunity to shape his environment. And shape his life.

CHERISHED MEMORIES

Don't let those family heirlooms gather dust! Use them; fill your life with the richness they add to any room. If I want to use an antique dresser scarf to line a tray—I just open a drawer in the kitchen, because they're right there ready to use. I keep my collection of favorite children's books on a shelf in the guest room—where overnight guests can enjoy them. And in our house, the teacups and teaspoons and other tea items that make up my collection are simply everywhere. When the grandchildren come over, we drink tea from them. I truly believe children are enriched by being entrusted with treasure. Treasures are better off when they're surrounded by everyday living. You'll be so much happier surrounded by beauty and memories.

OUT *of the* BOX

Paint your house orange? Well, maybe not! Most of us aren't in any danger of extremes when it comes to decorating. But try something a little unexpected. An oversized picture, a shelf hung lower than usual, a red pillow in a green room. It will do wonders for your decor. And by all means, mix styles, colors, and textures. It can be visually exciting. Just have a common element, such as color or design, to tie them all together. Try to get rid of those preconceived notions about what you "ought" to have in a room. Think instead about what you need. I say, "When in doubt—use it!"

LOVING YOUR LIFE

Fill your home with things that remind you of who you are—and what you love. I feel immediately at home in houses where people have surrounded themselves with what they love. It also gives us something to talk about. Don't you feel welcome and comfortable in a room that reflects the owner's personality? I feel the same way in my own rooms—because there's so much of me in them. A family photo album, Christmas ornaments handed down from generation to generation (yes, even in the spring!), books and signs and plaques collected on trips, a verse of Scripture. Somehow it all comes together to say, "This is who we are. This is what we love." The point of it all is making yourself and other people feel at home.

More Books for the Home and Heart from Emilie Barnes

CLEANING UP THE CLUTTER
Easy Ways to Keep Your Family Organized

Most women feel overwhelmed as they juggle raising a family, pursuing a career, and keeping a home. With great ideas supplemented by helpful organizational tools and charts, Emilie Barnes comes to the rescue and shows you how to...

- get the house clean and keep it that way
- involve family members in helping with chores
- plan healthful meals that save time and cut grocery bills

500 TIME-SAVING HINTS FOR EVERY WOMAN
Helpful Tips for Your Home, Family, Shopping, and More

In this easy-to-use resource, Emilie reveals 500 fabulous secrets to creating a life that has less mess and more room for what really matters, helping you

- declutter your life and home
- stop piling it and start filing it
- begin each day with a to-do list
- clean efficiently and effectively
- tackle projects at home and elsewhere

DESIGNING YOUR HOME ON A BUDGET
Knowing the Rules and How to Break Them All • Finding the Bargains • Loving the Results!

Revealing the keys to decorating beautifully on a budget, Emilie and Yoli provide basic design principles and ways to implement or break them to create a unique style. You'll discover how to do the things that establish a comfortable, inviting home, such as...

- adding little touches to liven up a room
- knowing when to refurbish and when to buy new
- finding affordable new and used treasures
- making a child's room fun

To read sample chapters of these books, go to www.harvesthousepublishers.com

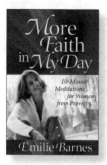

MORE FAITH IN MY DAY
10-Minute Meditations for Women from Proverbs

Emilie invites you to take a moment away from daily demands to rejuvenate your heart and mind with wisdom from Proverbs. *More Faith in My Day* offers the Bible's insights to your heart through features like...

- devotions inspired by Proverbs' teachings of goodness, love, work, family
- "Today's Wisdom" to enrich personal faith life
- ideas to turn God's abundant knowledge into action
- prayers for moments of meditation and connection

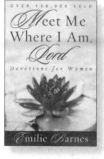

MEET ME WHERE I AM, LORD
Devotions for Women

In these short but thought-provoking meditations created especially for busy women, you can experience the lasting refreshment of God's presence meeting you...right where you are. Emilie Barnes offers...

- devotions to inspire and encourage
- practical suggestions for infusing life with faith
- closing prayers to place concerns in God's hands
- Bible verses for wisdom and comfort
- space to write reflections

A QUIET REFUGE
Prayers and Meditations for Hope and Healing

This selection of prayers and meditations offers you stepping-stones to a personal sanctuary. You'll discover restoration and hope in Kathleen Denis's paintings of inviting gardens, beckoning beachside chairs, and welcoming, sheltered spaces. Perfect for giving as a gift and for keeping within heart's reach, this collection offers you renewal for the journey and a quiet place to feel God's presence.

To read sample chapters of these books, go to www.harvesthousepublishers.com